PRAISE
By Land, Sky & Sea

"Parma weaves together Celtic, Faerie, and Balinese traditional understandings, augmented by Hellenic and Kemetic insights, and expanded by both firsthand Australian and European perspectives, to produce an innovative, comprehensive, essentially nonsectarian, pragmatic, and refreshing spiritual/magickal approach."

—Michael York, author of *Pagan Theology:*
Paganism as a World Religion

"A fascinating buffet of ideas and practices from many cultures and traditions, neatly packaged into a coherent system. Fresh and welcome material from the next generation of Pagan authors!"

—John J. Coughlin, author of *Ethics and the Craft*

"Gede Parma has created a unique book. There are very few books which discuss this subject, and nearly none that are just on spiritual cosmology alone. This book will be of use to anyone following the Pagan magical path—not just Witches but also Druids and Shamans. This is destined to be a classic."

—Janet Farrar and Gavin Bone,
authors of *Progressive Witchcraft*

"Witches, magicians, and spiritual individuals of all varieties can learn from the sound, intelligent, and experiential advice found in *By Land, Sky & Sea.* The mystical techniques and honest advice given in this book will be a much-needed inspiration for those who wish to deepen and actualize their living spirituality."

—Raven Digitalis, author of *Shadow Magick Compendium*
and *Planetary Spells and Rituals*

"A positive, proactive approach to Paganism both traditional and modern. Lyrical, anecdotal, and practical by turns, Parma creates a syncretic Celtic knot of traditional shamanism and diverse spiritual techniques. This book will engage and refresh the seasoned practitioner of modern Witchcraft and enlighten the novice equally. Recommended."

—Kala Trobe, author of *The Witch's Guide to Life*

Praise for
Spirited

"Woven through the writing is a treasure trove of visualizations, spells, and rituals that speaks to Parma's years of serious participation in the Pagan world."

—*New Age Retailer*

"Parma's book is knowledgeable, insightful, full of personal anecdotes, and laced with a passion and idealism that only comes with youth…this is a must-read for anyone who considers themselves a leader in the Pagan community or is working towards becoming a high priest or high priestess."

—TheMagicalBuffet.com

BY

LAND

SKY

&

SEA

ABOUT THE AUTHOR

Gede Parma is a Witch, initiated priest, and award-winning author. He is an initiate and teacher of the WildWood Tradition of Witchcraft, a hereditary healer and seer with Balinese-Celtic ancestry, and an enthusiastic writer. Gede is a keen student of natural health therapies, with a deep interest in herbal healing and nutrition, and he is currently studying for a bachelor's degree in health science. He is the proud partner of a beautiful Virgo man and the devoted priest of the goddesses Persephone, Aphrodite, and Hekate. His spiritual path is highly syncretic and incorporates elements of traditional shamanism, Balinese Hinduism, British-Celtic Witchcraft, Stregheria, Greek Paganism, Feri, Reclaiming, and WildWood Witchcraft.

Visit Gede at www.gedeparma.com.

BY

LanD

SKY

&

SEa

GEDE
PARMA

THREE REALMS OF SHAMANIC WITCHCRAFT

LLEWELLYN PUBLICATIONS
Woodbury, Minnesota

FIRST EDITION
First Printing, 2010

Cover art: forest—iStockphoto.com/Dmitry Mordvintsev
          wave—iStockphoto.com/Lachlan Currie
          sky—iStockphoto.com/Randy Plett Photographs
          flower—iStockphoto.com/Classix
Cover design by Kevin R. Brown

Llewellyn is a registered trademark of Llewellyn Worldwide Ltd.

Library of Congress Cataloging-in-Publication Data
Parma, Gede, 1988–
  By land, sky & sea : three realms of shamanic witchcraft / Gede Parma.
—1st ed.
    p. cm.
  Includes bibliographical references and index.
  ISBN 978-0-7387-2282-5
  1. Witchcraft. 2. Shamanism. I. Title. II. Title: By land, sky and sea.
  BF1566.P29 2010
  299´.94—dc22
                             2010021534

Llewellyn Publications
A Division of Llewellyn Worldwide Ltd.
2143 Wooddale Drive
Woodbury, MN 55125-2989

www.llewellyn.com
Printed in the United States of America

To my mother, Roslyn Farquharson,
for her subtle magick, her earthy wisdom,
and her Celtic blood. And to Essie Farquharson,
my mother's mother, who now walks in
the Land of Youth with her beloved Peter.

EDITOR'S NOTE

Readers may note that this book contains word spellings and phrasing unique to British English. These have been retained in order to honor the author's individual voice and spirit.

CONTENTS

PART ONE ☿ LAND

PART THREE ☿ SEA

acknowledgments

Thank-you to Ana and Awen for reminding me to breathe.

To Amy, beautiful Muireann, for organising my timetable.

To Eire for the blessed idea!

To Jarrah—bless Eris and her "piss-able" 8 card!

To Alex, who reminds me every now and then that I'm not a normal twenty-one-year-old…and I should be (sometimes).

To Becky for all that lemon sorbet and for the blessed sessions in the park!

To Luna la Fay and Queen Serpentine, who helped me reconnect with my Irish heritage.

To Elysia, who opened the door and helped me succeed.

To Becky Zins—you are an editor extraordinaire!

To the Witches of Earthwyrm for being guinea pigs.

To Luna, Arione, Meriel, Rowan, Serica, and Helona, who helped me gather together poignant quotes, and to all those who gave me their thoughts on initiation and what it means.

To the cunning rooster Lizz, the wonderful and radiant Mim, the cynical but hilarious Liz, the global-girl Fee, and to Alyce, Maddeline, and all the "work" girls (haha).

To Osiris, the crazy kitten; you brought hilarity when I needed it.

To Greg for loving me.

To all Wildkin who dance with me through the WildWood—may it flourish!

PReFACe

It should be noted that while this book is divided into three parts based on the Celtic three-realm cosmology of land, sky, and sea, there are methods, techniques, and ways drawn upon and acknowledged in this book that derive from different cultures and traditions. These cultures include (among others) Greek,[1] Hawaiian, Hindu, Stregheria, and Wiccan, and they will be referred to respectively at the appropriate time. This is done in the spirit of our Pagan forebears, who ventured into new spiritual and cultural frontiers with fervour, a keen heart, and a desire for wisdom. This tradition of weaving together, with purpose, a variety of cultural customs and religious traditions into a new spiritual whole is called syncretism, and the best-known historical example is the mostly Kemetic-Hellenic fusion that occurred in the Ptolemaic (Greek-ruled) city of Alexandria in northern Egypt in the fourth century BCE.

---

1 The spellings of all ancient Greek terms (including the names of the deities) will be true to the original forms of Greek. Thus, Dionysos and Orpheos end with "os" instead of "us," which is the Latinized variation. Similarly, Apollon ends with an "n," and Hekate and Eurydike substitute "k" for the Latin "c" usually found included in these names.

Despite my deep respect for tradition, I am also highly syncretic in my ways. I never impose on or misappropriate the various cultural and spiritual practices and traditions that I weave into my life; however, if my spirit is called by the Divine in one way or another, I will hearken to that call and follow it. This is the reason that I give reverence to deities from the Balinese, Celtic, Egyptian, and Mediterranean (Hellenic and Etruscan) pantheons. The former two are directly related to my ancestry, as my father is Balinese and my mother is of Celtic descent (Irish mostly, and Scottish), and the latter two, I believe, are connected to me because I have lived many lives in that area of the world devoted to those gods. As I have always been a highly devout person by nature, these gods have travelled with me through my multiple lives; for that, I am thankful.

I hope that this blending of cultures and traditions, as is the trend in Neopaganism, will not offend the stoic traditionalist or mislead the rampant eclectic who mixes and matches without thought or direction. Remember to always respect the origins of things and to honour your ancestors, for you are the outcome of your family's legacy.

For those of you who derive from a mostly Wiccan background or any Neopagan tradition that celebrates and honours the harmony and balance of the four elements (made whole by the spirit), please do not feel that the elements are in any way compromised by my focus on the three realms in this book. I do acknowledge the similarities in vibration between the land and earth, the sky and air, and the sea and water. This feeling, of course, would seem to negate fire. However, it has been theorised (and it feels right to me) that where the three realms meet, a fire is lit to mark the occasion with power and celebration and in reverence of the Divine—the wholeness achieved by union of the land, sky, and sea. The Celts were a fire-oriented society, and the four main Celtic holy days are known as the fire festivals, as each one involved the lighting of balefires.

Fire has been considered for millennia to be a gift from the gods. In fact, in some cultures, fire was said to be stolen from the gods (e.g., Prometheos of the Greek myths). Fire is such a powerful and transformative force that, when placed in the wrong hands, it can cause drastic and lasting effects. However, fire is also illumination, warmth, and the inspiration of the soul. All of this would make no sense without the world tree of shamanic cosmology.

The world tree joins the three realms and makes them whole. Its roots delve deep into the dark belly of the underworld, its trunk forms the physical reality of the middleworld, and its branches stretch high into the ether of the upperworld. The world tree embodies the totality of the cosmos, and its symbolism is cross-cultural. Examples of cultural and shamanic manifestations of the world tree include Yggdrasil of the Norse, the Mighty Bile or Greak Oak (of Uisneach, County Westmeath) of the Irish, the Moon Tree of the Assyro-Babylonian cultures, and Irminsul of the Anglo-Saxon people.[2]

It is generally believed that the world tree is a distinctly shamanic concept and that its relevance to any other tradition is moot. The world tree is a shamanic truth, and this would be a discrete thing had shamanism not formed the spiritual foundation for Paganism worldwide.

Witchcraft is a shamanistic spiritual tradition, and many of our ancient customs and practices are reflected in various indigenous shamanisms. For instance, during the persecution of Witches in Europe, many of the trial records document the folk tradition of villagers dancing around and dressing old trees with ribbon, cloth, and garlands. In fact, trees form a common theme in the Witch trials and highlight the continuance of ancient shamanic practice.

The world tree is at the centre of the universe. The centre is in all places, in all times. Thus, it does not matter whether we find ourselves nestled within the mighty roots of a towering oak or standing on the

2   Farrar and Bone, *Progressive Witchcraft*, 134.

shore, physically oriented between and wholly within all three realms. By the same token, you could simply visualise such a place and draw on that experience to guide your journeys. Essentially, you are the world tree; you are the joiner of the three realms, abiding within and sheltering them all simultaneously. You are the wandering centre that never ceases to be. May this book be a guide for your journeying, and may it inspire you to wander wisely, soar higher, and dive deeper. By land, by sky, by sea—by the ancient trinity—so mote it be!

INTRODUCTION

The twenty-first century is a bleak age. Political deceit, war, greed, famine, and environmental degradation are causing unrest even in the most conservative of societies. However, the Greening Tide of nature and the cosmic evolution of consciousness are inspiring hundreds of thousands of people to ponder and engage with the mysteries of life and our planet Earth. In doing so, many of us find the wisdom of our ancestral traditions, collectively known as Paganism (at least in the West), greatly illuminating.

In the Western mystery traditions, one culture has come to the fore of the romantic imagination, and this, of course, is that of the Celts. It is important to understand the differences between the Celtic reconstructionist philosophies and the decidedly more romanticised fusions of modern strains of Witchcraft with Celtic culture. Neither one is more spiritual than the other (or more authentic); however, it is in my personality and experience to emphasise and celebrate the correlations and commonalities between both. Each serves its purpose.

When exploring Celtic spirituality, it has been a popular trend to delve into the shamanistic aspects of its mystery traditions. This has demonstrated that despite the seas that divide us, the indigenous spiritualities all stem from a common source of divine inspiration and share many marked similarities. One similarity is perhaps the most significant: the threefold division of worlds. These worlds can be generically classified as the upperworld, the middleworld, and the underworld. The upperworld corresponds with the heavenly world of the gods—the Celtic sky. The middleworld is our physical earth, the plane of mortal manifestations—the Celtic land. The underworld is the home of the ancestors and the chthonic spirits that dwell inside the land—the Celtic sea.[3] In various shamanic cultures, there are various realms that exist within the three worlds respectively. In Norse cosmology, for example, there are three layers to each world.

When I first envisaged writing this book, I was travelling through Ireland with two close Pagan friends. On our journey through Eire, we had been communing with the land and the spirits of place at every given chance. Once inspired, an idea firmly consolidated itself in my mind: I felt it was time for a book that brought the simple beauty of Celtic mysticism to the global Pagan community in a way that would allow for a deepening of the soul and its awareness of the mysteries. I also decided that when I returned to Australia, I would run a series of weekend courses that presented my local Pagan community with a more intensive look at techniques and traditions that exhibited our shamanic roots and would revitalise the spirit.

By Land, Sky & Sea is an exploration of the Celtic ancient trinity with the goal of deepening one's Pagan spirituality and Craft, although I am quite sure non-Pagans will also find many hidden rewards within these pages.

---

3   In Celtic cultures, the otherworld lay beyond the sea, thus its correlation with the ancestors and underworld spirits.

This book is divided into three parts, each part named appropriately—Land, Sky, and Sea (of course!). Part One: Land deals with the fundamentals of earth spirituality. Breathwork, affirmations of self, being and body, grounding and centring, living in the now, and knowing the lay of the land are all considered basic 101 subjects; however, they are barely considered with a passing glance by the fast-tracking Pagan. It is integral to have a deep understanding of these key principles so that evolution and deeper understanding on the magickal path may inevitably occur.

In Part Two: Sky, I cover consciousness and energy—how to expand and articulate the former and work and weave with the latter. Spirit flight, clear sight (clairvoyance), and the intimate gifts of intuition are part and parcel of becoming at one with the energy, the life force, that courses through our universe. Instead of immanence, in working with the powers of the sky we delve into that alien concept of transcendence and how it is useful.

Part Three: Sea deals with the more commonly known shamanic talents, including trance, vision journeying, channeling, and receiving oracles. In many Celtic myths, the sea is the portal to the otherworld; therefore, it is fitting that these primal techniques are covered in this part.

It is my keen desire that this book be a helpful directive for those Pagans interested in deepening their spirituality and being rid of the limitations that impinge on their everyday perceptions. This book is not only for those of the priesthood (whatever the tradition or vocation)—this is a book for all those who wish to explore what we now call shamanism under the guise of the Neopagan traditions and to enhance and sharpen their own magickal abilities.

May the land rise up to meet you, may the all-encompassing sky bless you, and may the sea that surrounds and lies within keep you in its infinity. By land, by sky, by sea—blessed be!

tHe shamanic witch

As in the way of the shaman, so in the way of the witch.
—Ly de Angeles, *Witchcraft: Theory and Practice*

Witchcraft is innately a shamanic tradition. Perhaps Witchcraft is merely a European name for the spiritual equivalent of the indigenous medicine people the world over. The word *shaman* itself derives from the Siberian Tungus dialect (*saman*) and refers specifically to a Tungus medicine healer. Of course, anthropologically and spiritually speaking, these medicine people exist in almost every indigenous culture. At the core of all of these "shamanisms" lies the same wisdom teaching—the universe/world/mystery is alive, and it is right and respectful to interact purposefully with it. The outcome of these facilitated interactions is a relationship engendered through a trust of the spirits (the Divine), which will then serve and benefit a community of beings. The various traditions of modern Witchcraft weave the mystic journey for oneness with the All and desire to aid the community of beings within place and time. A Witch has always been a friend to the elemental spirits of nature, and thus, through this working relationship, a Witch is empowered to communicate with the spirits/gods/forces to create desired change or to delve into the mysteries of the time. Of course, there is so much more to Witchcraft than spellcraft and divination, but the methodologies and talents of the Craft arise from the primal experience of the world as animate and thus responsive.

Shamanic Witchcraft is an overloaded phrase, and I'm not so sure it's an entirely useful one. In a world such as ours, perhaps it is necessary to differentiate the Neo-Wiccan[4] practices from the primal, ecstasy-driven, celebratory inclinations of nature-mystic Witchcraft. This book is specifically aimed at those people who consciously aim to resurrect and enliven the deeper shamanic aspects of the Craft and therefore desire to develop the talents associated with these teachings to do so.

---

4   Neo-Wicca is a term that is sometimes used in the Pagan community to distinguish the older Wiccan mystery traditions from the diluted, self-help New Age emphases given in many handbooks today.

WITChCRAFT: A NEW DEFINITION[5]

Perhaps it is time that we redefine the term *Witchcraft*. In and of itself (technically speaking), the concept and phenomenon of Witchcraft will always be, to academics at least, the exercise of the magickal arts to attain and fulfil personal and communal desires. The traditions, methods, and rituals one employs to do so may differ in each case study according to cultural context and locale; however, in its essence, Witchcraft implies magick. However, what does Witchcraft mean to those who practise its arts today? Are we a religious group purposely allying ourselves with the old Pagan customs and traditions? Are we philosophers who delight in obscuring the fine lines delineating sects and spiritual groups? Or are we simply a group of people who, with wit and a touch of universal ingenuity, seek self-gratification above all? Perhaps all—and perhaps none—of the above.

I offer a new definition of Witchcraft to the Pagan community. I do not expect or desire that it be implemented as the ultimate definition above all others; I simply wish to offer insight into what we are as Witches in a world that would otherwise cast us aside with cynicism or downright self-righteous zeal. The definition I offer others, when asked what Witchcraft is to me, is this: "Witchcraft is an ecstasy-driven, earth-based mystery path (or paths)."

Witchcraft has been, throughout the ages, many different things to many different people. Anthropologically speaking, a Witch is an individual who dwells on the fringe of society in that they practise a sorcery not wholly accepted as benevolent by society. This can be seen quite obviously within some traditional African tribal communities who revere and honour the local shaman (for lack of a better term) as a healer and oracle to the spirits, and who detest the sorcerer as a foul and evil Witch perpetually bent on weaving malice in the community. However, this says nothing for truth and everything for perception. Therefore, in reclaiming the stigmatised word *Witch*, we must not seek it out in how we are viewed by others through ignorance but

---

5   This article was first published in Issue 9 of Australia's *Spellcraft* magazine. It is reprinted here with permission.

in the pure sense of nature, where, etymologically speaking, there are some interesting clues.

The argument for the origins of the word *Witch* has been raging for decades; however, despite what many people (including renowned Witches) would have us believe, the most historically viable root is the Indo-European word *weik*,[6] which refers to religio-magick. A religio-magickal tradition is one that, in the eyes of academics, blends spirituality with the magickal arts. However, Witches and Pagans are not so dualistic in this interpretation, in that we do not perceive magick to be divorced from spirituality and vice versa; they are of the same and are one. In the generic Pagan view, magick is the very essence of nature, and nature is the very foundation of our spirituality, therefore one cannot be separate from the other; it would be senseless and ignorant to think so. A Witch, in the Pagan context at least, is one who honours nature as divine expression (immanence) and who weaves the energies of the natural world into rhythmic pulses of life sent forth with intent and impassioned desire to effect change in the apparent/seen world through the unseen planes; in this, we are shamanistic. The etymological origins of the word *Witch* make it clear that Witches have always been spiritual folk who desire to deepen their relationship with the natural world and the universe, which is as the microcosm to the macrocosm.

To further clarify, what I mean by Witchcraft is that I do not mean Wicca. Wicca, in its original form, is a Pagan religion that was either founded or made accessible through the late Gerald Brosseau Gardner. Its ceremonies and three-degree initiatory rites of admission

---

6   Raven Grimassi, in *The Witches' Craft* (USA: Llewellyn, 2002), cites the historian Jeffrey B. Russell, who gives the Indo-European root *weik* as the etymological ancestor to the word *witch* (*A History of Witchcraft*, Thames and Hudson Ltd., 1980). The word *weik* refers to both religion and magick, in the primal sense of which it was originally used—meaning that if religion was mentioned, magick was implied, and vice versa, as there is no true separation between the two. Russell goes on to state that *weik* gave birth to *wih-l*, which the Old English word *wigle* derives from, meaning "sorcery."

and elevation are clearly Masonic in many aspects, although there is retained within them a true sense of morphic resonance (as Frederic Lamond put it so eloquently in his book *Fifty Years of Wicca*) that suggests earlier throwbacks. The Gardnerian tradition celebrates the esbats (at the full moon) and the eight solar high days we call the sabbats, and honours both a horned god and a lunar goddess. It is an oath-bound initiatory tradition whose practitioners, in my experience, are extremely devout and often very pragmatic. However, not all Witches are Wiccan, and interestingly enough, not all Wiccans claim to be Witches, though their religious rituals are inherently magickal (e.g., the casting of the circle).

The Witchcraft I practise both within my coven and on my own does not follow a religious vein. I am deeply spiritual, but I refuse to align myself with the lexicon of religion based on its current-day affiliations with orthodox, mainstream organisations and its etymological roots (i.e., the Latin *religare*, "to bind back"). The most obvious indicator of corrupt religion is hidebound dogma and its institutionalisation. This has occurred throughout history; however, it is most obvious in current-day monotheistic faiths (e.g., Christianity and Islam). It must be made clear, however, that the majority of the adherents to these faiths are, in fact, level-headed spiritual beings who simply seek a relationship with the Divine. Witches, too, seek personal relationships with the Divine; however, we do not necessarily view it as transcendent and detached from the material plane—in fact, we view it as wholly a part of it.

If a non-religious Witchcraft can exist (and it does), how is it reconciled with those in the Pagan community who view themselves as practising a religion? The Pagan community is decentralised, autonomous, and largely anarchistic—we have no authoritarian ruling body that passes edicts over us, therefore there are no problems with diversity (and it flourishes!). If one chooses to look at history's representation of Witchcraft—and, of course, the truths that lie behind these perceptions—a vivid story unfolds: a story steeped in shadow and secrecy; dancing in groves, skyclad bodies shimmering under the radiance of the full moon; perfect love and perfect trust; Old Ones and spirits of place; parting the veil and dwelling between. We are truly denizens of an otherworldly lineage; if only we all knew how otherworldly this earth is. This is not supernatural—it's merely an expansion of consciousness that reveals something beyond the mundane drudgery we live through day to day. There are patterns and symbols, cycles and rhythms. Witches work to attune themselves to these natural forces and tides, therefore becoming whole and at one with the Pure Will, where destiny unfolds.

We have been called the myrk-riders, the hedge witches, the cunning folk, and the medicine men and women. It is because we do not deny the mystery its way (nor could we) that we are therefore the priesthood of the Old Ways, which imbue the individual with power. This is the kind of power that does not require coercion or domination, but rather is pure and wilful intent balanced with spiritual grace and infused with the rhythmic breath of life. Witches are heirs to a great source of power. We call it magick, though others have different names for it—fate, luck, chance, coincidence. It is this force that underlies all things that reminds us of the paradox we honour. Are time and its events preordained by an omnipotent deity, or are all things created by cause and effect? The Witch would say, "No, not all things are set in stone," and again, "No, we must remember fate," and then perhaps she would wink slyly and say, "It's all a memory of something—past, present, future—the spiral of the holy continuum, a blink in the great eye of She Who Is All," and be done.

So, once again, Witchcraft—as I experience it—is an ecstasy-driven, earth-based mystery path. Ecstasy-driven because we yearn for the Self beyond the self that is, in truth, more than the sum of its parts and equal to it, and we perform rituals harnessing powerful techniques of trance to attain this. Earth-based because without her, who are we?

The Earth is the Mother from whom we rose, and it is to her we shall return. We are her rhythm, her cycle; if out of balance, we destroy not only her, but ourselves. We are mysterious because the great mystery is never known beyond that which she gives to behold—and in that glimmer of her is the All, and that is the mystery. We are Witches because inherent in the world is magick, and it flows through us all. Magick doesn't happen; it *is*.

LAND

PART
ONE

CORRESPONDENCES

Classical Element	Earth
Shamanic World	Middleworld
Themes	Being in the now (presence), comfort, home, interconnection & interdependency, labour/work, mother, nourishment, resilience, sacrifice, seasons, solidarity, sovereignty, sustenance
Cultural/Esoteric Symbols	Crops of the harvest, the dish/plate, flowers/offerings, the lia fail of the gifts of the Tuatha De Danann, the pentacle of the Craft tools, the Sovereign Queen of western European mythos
Herbs/Plants	Alfalfa, barley, copal, corn, cotton, cypress, fern, mugwort, oleander, patchouli, potato, primrose, rye, sage, tulip, vervain, vetiver, wheat, wood sorrel
Colours	Black, brown, green, red (ochre)

1

TO BREATHE

Live each season as it passes; breathe the air, drink the drink,
taste the fruit, and resign yourself to the influences of each.
—Henry David Thoreau

When we are born, we take in our first breath of life, and before we die, we let go of our last. We are sustained by this delicate mixture of oxygen and nitrogen throughout our physical incarnations on this Earth. It is this rhythm of rising and falling, propelled by a beating heart, that our body follows and dances to. The way we breathe can also affect our consciousness, in turn altering our perceptions. It is this secret art of breath control that allows the magickal person to achieve other states and to transform one's relationship with the energy of life—what I call magick.

The breath of life is not only a metaphor for what we undeniably need, but it is also a story that whispers of impassioned moments of touching the divine heartthrob of the mystery itself. It is not a coincidence that when we are awed by something, our breath catches, and we gasp. For that infinite moment, we are the breath of life—so intimately a part of it that we no longer need to physically breathe (or so I would like to think).

The Latin word for breath is *anima*. Interestingly, anima also means "soul," and the late psychologist Carl Jung made it one of his nine dominant archetypes when he said that the Anima was the indwelling feminine spirit within a man. Thus, Anima can be seen to be that force of life that sustains us—our soul, our breath, the Mother. This chapter will explore the importance of breathwork in Pagan traditions and the various methods of consciously breathing. Let's begin.

CONSCIOUS BREATHWORK

The Yogic Breath

In the Eastern art of yoga (and Witchcraft has been called the yoga of the West), one is taught a simple method for conscious breathing. This involves breathing deeply in through the nose and exhaling through the mouth. This technique has come to be called the yogic breath and will form the basis of the breathwork that follows.

The Breath of Light

This technique of conscious breathing utilises the gifts of visualisation. When inhaling, one visualises white light (or another suitable colour like blue or silver) entering the body through the crown, and as the breath is drawn down into the abdomen, the light is seen and felt to pervade every cell, inundating the body with vitality and magick. On the exhalation, smoky, grey energy is seen/felt exiting the body. This visualisation affirms to the individual that all negativity is leaving the body and being transformed by the cosmos so that it can be breathed in again. Always make sure that your breaths are long and deep, so as to instill a peaceful state of being, and do not be afraid to allow the abdomen to expand to its fullest when you breathe in. Embrace the contraction when you exhale. In breathwork, the aim is to be rid of extraneous thoughts. If you are letting thoughts distract you, then you are not properly prepared for your purpose. Remember this when using any method of conscious breathing. However, do not become anxious if your mind becomes riddled with thoughts as you practise your breathing. Simply acknowledge each thought in passing, then let them go.

The breath of light helps to energise the body prior to magickal workings. It is useful before any kind of ritualistic or healing work. You can even adjust the colour of light to suit your magickal intent and purpose—for example, green light for healing and prosperity, or red for passion and love.

The "Ha" Huna Breath

This conscious-breathing method derives from the shamanic Huna traditions of Hawaii. I have been using this technique for several years now, and I find it highly effective in reining in my focus and energising my being for magickal work.

When "ha" breathing, I utilise visualisation just as with the breath of light, except I visualise white light both entering *and* leaving my body. I also see the light of my exhalation circulate to loop back and enter my crown as I breathe in. The "ha" itself is expressed on the exhalation. When breathing out, make a *haaaa* sound aloud (or silently if you prefer). The "ha" itself helps to direct the energy in a focussed manner.

This method of conscious breathing helps to centre, cleanse, and revitalise your aura, as well as align all "selves."[7]

The Counting/Square Breath

When I first began making meditation a pointed practice in my spirituality, I referred to Ray Buckland's "big blue book" (aka *Buckland's Complete Book of Witchcraft*), and that is where I learnt what I call the counting, or square, breath.

---

7 When I speak of the "selves," I imply that the wholeness we each are is multidimensional and comprised of various "functional" selves that manifest themselves as layers of consciousness (e.g., the threefold Feri division of the "self" as younger self, talking self, and deep self).

There are many ways to count your breaths. The square method that I employ is broken into four parts. Counting to four slowly, I breathe in; I then hold that breath for four counts. I exhale, counting to four, and then once again hold for four counts. This method can be used to deepen the stillness of the techniques listed above. In general, the counting breath aids in dispelling thoughts and focussing the mind.

These are the four primary breath techniques that I use in my practice. Each one builds on its predecessor, adding detail and definition.

Conscious breathing redirects one's focus to a state of being that underlies the frenetic comings and goings of mundane reality. It is a simple technique that restores one's equilibrium and vitality. This is necessary for intense magickal work, as it requires high levels of energy.

Another kind of breathwork that is extremely helpful in developing stillness and peace with the self is the art of observing one's breath. This is as simple as becoming aware of the way one breathes and watching it for a period of time. However, it must be said that many people in this fast-paced, urbanised world breathe rapidly and shallowly. This can lead to an array of physical health problems, not to mention that these kinds of breaths are not conducive to serious magickal work.

Practice

Find a quiet place and set aside at least half an hour daily for four days in which you can practice each of these methods respectively, building and adding to each one as you go along. On the fourth day, you should be able to meld all four together into one syncretised conscious breath technique. Inhaling through the nose, exhaling through the mouth, visualising a loop of white light as you do so. "Ha" on your exhalation, and remember to count your breaths to beats of four. Soon enough, personalised methods will arise through your continued practice of these four basic techniques.

2

TO GROUND AND CENTRE

*Feel the pulse of the earth beneath you. Sit on the
ground. Touch it. Run your fingers through the soil.
Build a relationship with the living earth.*
—Christopher Penczak, *The Temple of Shamanic Witchcraft*

Before beginning a ritual in Neopaganism, it is considered essential
to ground and centre, or at least to still the mind. Over the years, the
famous tree of life alignment meditation (and there are a variety!) has
proven the most effective in achieving the desired state of consciousness over the years. This chapter will explore the how-to (the technique itself) and the why of the tree of life alignment meditation. It is
hoped that the efficacy of this method will prove evident and that you,
the reader, will more deeply understand the reason for this practice
today.

Before I provide you with the meditation word for word, I would
like to add that I have found grounding and centring to be a useful
practice in almost any situation. When travelling in Europe recently,
I would ground and centre whenever we reached "new" land to formally acquaint myself with it. For example, after we disembarked the

ferry from Wales to Ireland, we drove a short way to Our Lady's Island in the very southeast of Ireland, and I aligned myself there with the tree of life, also called the world tree. My roots delved far into the belly of the Mother, and my branches stroked the canopy of the star-strung heavens. Previously, I had felt a little lacklustre, but immediately after grounding and centring, I felt rooted in place and felt my purpose burn brightly anew. I also find this practice helpful in situations of conflict or when I feel a little sick, deflated, or disorientated in general. Starhawk teaches the method to activists who put themselves on the front line and finds that these methods aid in calming a person and bringing them into harmony with their surroundings. An individual "realises" and therefore proves powerful and in control in circumstances that usually break down morale.

THE TREE OF LIFE ALIGNMENT MEDITATION

Below, you will find what I have called the tree of life alignment meditation, which is really a fancy way of defining a method for grounding and centring. This method is particular to the WildWood Tradition of Witchcraft, of which I am an initiated priest and co-founder. Feel free to try it as it is or adapt it to your own tastes.

PART ONE—*Begin by closing your eyes and opening yourself to the sounds and rhythms all around you. As you breathe deeply in, you realise that these sounds form patterns and are, in truth, in harmony with one another. Delve deeper into the pattern to find the rhythm that inspires it. Let this rhythm be that of your breath as you inhale and exhale, breathing in the white light of the universe and releasing, as you exhale, all the stresses and anxieties of the day. You are here, in the now.*

PART TWO—*Now focus on your feet (or the base of your spine—whatever body part is touching the ground), and feel and see strong roots pushing through the layers of soil and earth, through the veins of minerals and chthonic water, until they reach the heart of the Mother herself. The molten heart-fire from this sacred place rushes up your roots and into your body, where it settles there as the dark earth light of the Mother, grounding and nurturing.*

PART THREE—*Now focus on your crown. In your mind's eye, your body is, in fact, the trunk of an ancient tree, and your consciousness now follows the path of your woven branches into the sky realms. Here, the bright white light of the heavens enters your branches like lightning, like quicksilver, and pours into your body, mixing with the dark earth energy. They meet and marry and are one within you, as they always have been. You are their child—a mighty pillar between heaven and earth. Blessed be.*

I will now deconstruct each of the three parts of the meditation and explain why they are as they are.

Part One is the initiation of the flow of energy. By closing one's eyes and attuning to the rhythms in nature, you will find a solace and equilibrium that cleanses your being and reaffirms it as part of the intricate (and simple) pattern of life. The breathwork here is obvious and draws upon colour visualisation—white, to instill peace and clarity—and of course the yogic breath, which is useful in hollowing out the mind, ridding it of thought, and establishing a pure rhythm that the conscious mind may follow at leisure. On every exhalation, one may purposefully and powerfully banish the mundane drivel of the day and breathe in peace and at-one-ment with the universe. Part One ends with a succinct affirmation of being in the present and relaxing, without fear, into it.

Part Two brings the focus to the Earth that is our foundation—the land itself! In projecting one's consciousness (through energetic roots) into the womb of the Goddess, we find ourselves experiencing the raw physicality of our Mother—a manifestation of divinity. Knowing the land you live on can help you have a more in-depth experience with grounding, in that you can more vividly picture in your mind what it is exactly your roots are travelling through. Judy Harrow paints this picture beautifully when she says in her book *Devoted To You*, "Lately, some Pagans have been creating geologically accurate grounding meditations. Instead of talking generically about soil, water table, and bedrock, these meditations describe the actual rock strata in your area, and also a bit about how those particular rocks were formed." After penetrating the dark mysteries of the earth, we come to Gaia's own heart. Our roots receive the earth-fire and absorb it into the trunk of the tree—your body. This not only energises the body and prepares it for the intensity of magickal work ahead, it also firmly grounds you in the physical plane, our source for all bodily nourishment.

Part Three centres on receiving and drawing down the light of the sky realms, and it ends with the sealing of both heaven and earth coming together as one within your body (your being) as the pillar that unites the two. Your consciousness flows through your branches as you mentally extend them into limitless space, and there, stroking infinity, they receive the divine charge of the sky realms, what we perceive to be transcendent. Our experiences in this plane of reality tend to be of a revelatory nature simply because we are unused to the extremely high vibration of the energy that exists there. Once our own vibration synchronises with the energy of the sky, we become a part of the revelation that is the All—the great mystery of life. When the white light of the heavens and the dark light of the earth meet, they marry, drawn together enigmatically, as magnetic opposites attract and come together by their very natures. The grounding and centring has thus actualised itself within your being, and you are focussed and prepared for whatever work lies ahead of you.

As mentioned above, grounding and centring has become a prerequisite ritual practice for most Pagans today, especially those who blend the newer variants of Pagan spirituality with the older traditions. We do not know if, historically speaking, the Old Ones prepared themselves similarly, as not much of our Pagan European culture was recorded so forthrightly; we need to be able to read the subtle signs they have left for us in the landscape and in myth. However, in my experience, Paganism and its rites are nature-derived, and this means nature as it encompasses all things, including our humanity. Humans often take deep breaths naturally before committing themselves to a physical act or even when making a significant decision in life. I believe that we do this to clear our minds and focus our energies—in other words, to ground and centre.

In my book *Spirited: Taking Paganism Beyond the Circle,* I talk about giving and receiving in equal measure in my chapter on ritual. I refer to the need to always keep in mind what one is sending out versus what one is receiving. Basically, we need to give to get, and vice versa. If not, our energy sources become depleted, and we could end up in mental disarray, etheric unease, or physical illness. Also, if one is raising power towards a specific goal and all they have called upon is their own personal power, the effects will not materialise as strongly as it would had that person drawn upon nature's abundant life force.

Grounding and centring helps to align oneself with the powers of nature as expressed specifically through a "joiner" of heaven and earth. The tree of life, or the world tree, is both a symbol and a reality (the former reflecting the latter). With our roots firmly in the ground and our branches painting the skies, we are whole in all realms, for the world-encircling "stream" (the great sea/ocean) is what nourishes our roots and inspires our dreaming.

Practice

In sacred space, at your altar or wherever, practice the tree of life alignment, and make sure you engage your entire being with the task at hand. Transcend physical limitations and allow yourself truly to be the world tree. When you visualise, you are giving form to an energy that is ever-present, and if fed with conviction and intent, these forms will direct and shape this energy, moulding them to our wills.

To flesh out the technique, research the geology of your area more completely, and integrate your findings into your visualisations when grounding and centring.

3

TO LOVE THE BODY

The body is the temple.
—Unknown

The body is of matter, and the word *matter* comes from the Latin *mater*, meaning "mother." The Mother and the Feminine have always been considered, at least in the Western mystery traditions, to be of the physical, of matter. Perhaps this is because the woman is considered to be more closely connected with the physical world, as she is the one who births the spirit into this world of form, and she is also the one whose body flows with the cycles of nature, specifically those of the moon. In saying this, it must be remembered that all things in this world (that thing we call nature) are expressions of spirit, and spirit is an expression of nature; the child mirrors the parent as the parent reflects the child. Therefore, we cannot simply cast woman as the physical entity without considering woman as a spiritual, mental, and emotional being also. I speak from a man's point of view, albeit one who shamelessly and with great mirth honours the Great Mother.

Before I speak of the body and its significance both to the land (as that is what the land is) and to Paganism, I wish to speak of the Mother, or what most Neopagans call the Goddess. For many years I have struggled with this concept purely because I came from a Wiccan background[8] and could only see her through that lens. Most eclectic forms of Wicca describe the Goddess as being an overarching supernal Mother figure who encompasses within herself all goddesses. The God is described similarly. However, as a queer male, and one who experiences sexuality and gender as fluid, this philosophy has never sat well with me, purely because I do not agree that because a goddess is seen to be "female," they all must be of the Great Female Deity. This is ludicrous! The gods defy gender. We say *god* and *goddess* to describe various deities because we are human and wish to make the Divine more comprehensible to the human psychology, which has been conditioned by duality.

It was after I visited Glastonbury Tor that I became enlightened to the Goddess as the land, as the world, as all of humanity knows her—Mother Nature. Mother Nature has been identified with many deities throughout history; however, she is as she is, and I honour her for that. I have called her Gaia, but nowadays I prefer to simply think of her as one of the Old Ones, unnamed and deep. She is the sacred landscape, the body of the Divine.

The body is sacred! It is one of the many truths I experience daily. My strong belief in this truth is the reason I am vegan, the reason I rarely use pharmaceutical drugs, and the reason I do not smoke or partake of synthesised drugs. I do drink alcohol, but only wine.

---

8   I was born to a devout Balinese Hindu father and a highly intuitive mother; however, I began to explore the Craft and the Wiccan traditions when I was twelve. I am now an initiated priest of the WildWood Tradition and a Witch who weaves ancestry with the inspiration of the spirit. I do not identify myself as a Wiccan.

This is part of a geis[9] that I placed on myself several years ago. When I was in high school and somewhat of a rebel (in that stereotypically teenage sense), I made a dumping ground of my body at every party I attended. I smoked and drank myself sick, and my body made a point of always rejecting these toxins rather theatrically. It was almost two years before I took the hint. I then committed myself to a huge detox that is now an integral part of my life. The body is sacred, yes! Write down these words or something like them and place them in constant view so that you can truly absorb their meaning. Live these words and say them as a sacred prayer to the Goddess who is.

The Pagan traditions do not reject the material; we embrace the Mother, for she is Spirit incarnate. I was once discussing this principle of Paganism with a teacher who was a Pagan and a friend of mine at high school, and she said to me that nature is the perfect expression of the Divine. In contrast to Abrahamic faiths, which traditionally see the physical as something to bind and repress, Paganism celebrates what is inherently sacred. We are truly pantheists and animists. We value the spirit that animates the world and all within it. This is highly important and must be deeply understood before one can truly call oneself Pagan. We do not strive to move beyond this plane into an ethereal fantasy realm. We are here as children of the Great Mother, and we love the Goddess we call Earth. The body is sacred; it is divine.

The following sections will detail the finer points of integrating body wisdom into your life.

---

9   A geis (pronounced *gay-sh*) is a Celtic custom and can mean a vow that is binding. It can be placed upon you by another (somewhat like a curse), or it can be self-imposed. Once a geis is placed, it must not be broken, and those that do break a geis do so in full knowledge of the repercussions that may ensue.

TO DANCE

The Goddess is dancing!
—Pagan bumper sticker

I find that dancing lends itself to the passion of raising the
Kundalini, of freeing the soul to journey into the sphere of the Divine.
—Yasmine Galenorn, *Crafting the Body Divine*

I was a dancer long before I began to consciously engage with my spirituality. Some of the earliest pictures of me that my parents have are of me dancing, dressed in traditional Balinese dance costumes. I have always intuitively understood rhythm and music to be highly sacred and important to who I am and what I do, and indeed I believe them to be cornerstones of the Pagan traditions. When I dance, I am free.

In high school, I was a dancer in a contemporary youth dance theatre called Fringe. My teacher and friend, one of the most amazing people I have had the pleasure to know, saw dance as an expression of the soul and shared with us the meaning and methods of such a philosophy (see interview with Kirsty, page 21). I learnt much from her about what it is to be a creative practitioner, and much of what I picked up I have integrated into my living path.

In the ancient past, Paganism was not merely a group of people who came together regularly and officially to honour the seasons or practise other rites to attune with nature; the old Paganisms were cultures unto themselves. A Pagan was a Pagan because they were of a people, of a place, of a way of life that had developed organically over thousands of years, from Palaeolithic times into the Classical era and beyond. It was part of growing up to know the sacred arts of dance, drama, prayer, and ritual; these things were common heritage, and we have all but lost it. However, these old ways can and must be recovered and reclaimed. When I dance, it is part of my reclaiming.

In modern Witchcraft communities today, there are several traditional methods of dance we employ to help raise power in our rituals.

The most popular is the legendary spiral dance. The basic technique is this:

All are holding hands in a circle, and the person who will be leading the spiral dance breaks with the person on their left or right, depending on which direction the spiral will be moving—deosil or widdershins. Generally it is thought best to always dance deosil (with the sun), as this encourages growth and life. In the Northern Hemisphere, this would be clockwise. In the Southern Hemisphere, deosil is anti-clockwise; therefore, the leader in the Southern Hemisphere would break off from the person on their right. The leader then begins to move deosil, and all are following in tow. The spiral winds tighter and tighter, forming concentric circles from "row" to "row," until the leader reaches the centre. From here, the leader will turn back on him- or herself and then take the spiral in the opposite direction—widdershins. This can be repeated several times over. At the right moment, the power is released by dropping hands and throwing arms into the air. An emotive vocalisation always helps to encourage the power on its way.

Other forms of modern Pagan dance are simple enough. Go to any drumming circle or big Pagan event, and sure enough you will find fire (either in bonfire or fire-toy form) and drummers spurring on a group of entranced Pagans releasing inhibition and expressing the gift of rhythm. Low, grounded movements are popular and embody the close connection between us and the earth. African dance is a fine proponent of these kinds of movements. Acrobatic styles are also touched on and express the wild Fey nature possessed by many a Pagan. Unfortunately, in the Neopagan community at least, many of the older cultural dances have been ignored or lost, and not much work has been done on revitalising or restoring these old dances. However, it is important that this work is done and that the old ways are reclaimed, for there is much to be learnt from the ways of our ancestors.

Shamanism has been described as a "technique of ecstasy."[10] A major component of any shamanic tradition is dance, and it is used primarily as a method to transcend the ego—to *ek stasis*, stand outside (of oneself). In attaining this altered state of consciousness, we are freed from the mundane constrictions that keep us submissive and static, and thus we embrace change—the Universal Law. Once outside the discrete self one knows as "identity," everything becomes self. This teaching is central to the Vedic Upanishads. Through dance, one can be absorbed into the All of nature and the cosmos; one becomes the dance of life itself. One becomes entranced in the dance; it can lead to self-hypnosis. In Bali, many dancers are put into trances by priests before ceremonial dances take place. Having witnessed these dances myself, I can personally attest to the beauty and grace exhibited by the young, entranced dancers; it is almost as if little gods have decided to manifest before the village and express their divinity. In many cultures, dance is used to tell stories and to physically embody myth and legend. In this way, raw matter is used to convey the sacred that infuses all things. As highly visual and tactile beings, we can respond dramatically to such performances, and thus we are more likely to receive the messages and teachings they seek to impart.

In the Neopagan community, dance is mainly used either to raise power in ritual or to celebrate the body and its inherent sexuality. I have described the popular spiral-dance method of raising power above; however, free-form dance to appropriate music is just as effective. I often dance to music by Enigma, Loreena McKennitt, Santana, Wendy Rule, and tribal drumming tracks. These aural aids enhance my experience and often lead me into realms and states of being that are hard to put into words, though as a writer I attempt to! I highly recommend looking through your own music. You might discover something just right!

---

10 Mircea Eliade, the late Romanian historian and philosopher, described shamanism as a "technique of ecstasy" in *Shamanism: Archaic Techniques of Ecstasy* (USA: Bollingen Paperback Printing, 1972).

When dancing to celebrate the body in its divine glory (which can be done while raising power), perhaps you could end/ground with orgasm. Just like the act of sex itself, dance releases endorphins; thus, dance can be a form of foreplay! It makes absolute sense when you think about it. Some of the most rewarding, ecstatic sexual experiences I have ever had have followed long nights of clubbing. Yasmine Galenorn, a prolific Pagan author, says that dance, in her experience, releases the Kundalini energy. Kundalini, a Sanskrit term, refers to the serpentine energy that is coiled at the base of one's spine. It can rise, and when it does, it is said to bring enlightenment and freedom from mortal/mundane constraints. Actualising one's immediate divinity and entering the realm of the gods reminds us that we, ourselves, are their children, and therefore the divine "blood" flows through us. It is hard not to feel beautiful and good when this knowledge becomes ours. Just like the old temple priestesses of Inanna and Aphrodite, through dance we become the Goddess who is dancing and simultaneously give her the worship she so desires.

If you are interested in studying the art of dance, look into the contemporary dance movement and research the various styles that have evolved over the decades. Contemporary dance is dance at its most expressive. It exists at either side of the technique spectrum—highly articulated or deeply intuitive, and most times both. Look into choreographers like Isadora Duncan (who resurrected the grace and poise of the art of dance), Martha Graham (the myth-inspired choreographer whose heart was pulled by the ancient Greek tragedies), and Twyla Tharp (the mistress of flair, ferocity, and finesse), and pay close attention to the way these dancers describe what they do (or did) and why they do it.

If there are any multicultural festivals or events occurring in your area, make sure you pay a visit. You may stumble across a performance that triggers something primal within you. Many dances performed today exist in the same (or similar) form they have for centuries. In

Bali, the art of dance is considered to be delicately spiritual, and many dances are performed as offerings to the gods and spirits. To encounter these special moments of cultural heritage and passion is something to delight in! I feel blessed to have been born into it.

When I was younger, I used to accompany my mother and the musical group she played in (a performing Balinese gamelan, or orchestra) to the Australian Woodford Folk Festival,[11] which is held annually the week leading up to New Year's Day. I used to do a lot of solitary exploring through the festival, as I liked to observe the wild magick of the playful hippies and the different-looking folk who seemed to drink from a wellspring of perpetual happiness. I remember discovering so many hidden dance revels. There were the trancers swaying to the technotastic beats of underground DJs and the wild drum-dance sessions held in the infamous chai tent. Sometimes I just stood at the edges of the crowd, keenly watching the dancers and the dance, but when the mood struck and spirit called, I answered—I let go and let in the gods. Many people call this state of being transcendence, and Yasmine Galenorn has aptly described it as an "out-of-body/in-body" experience. However, what if these extreme expansions of consciousness were meant to happen here, in the now, in the body, with the Goddess—what if these experiences weren't mystic accidents? Some Witches see the Goddess, the sovereignty that is our Divine Source, as both immanent and transcendent. I have called her the Paradox Woman. Others call her the Dancing Goddess. I think a Goddess who dances is truly balanced within herself. I am honoured to be her child.

The physical act of dancing produces endorphins that, like sex and exercise, stimulate intense feelings of bliss and ecstasy within the body and thus within the spirit. Dance is a way to enlightenment! Consider for a moment the whirling dervishes of the Sufi tradition. Sufis believe

---

11 For more information on the Woodford Folk Festival, visit www.woodfordfolk festival.com.

(and experience) that their method of dance opens their minds and hearts to Allah (the Great Spirit/Creator). One could choose to see this as the Sufis realising through their rituals that they are no longer dancers, but the dance itself—and what else is the dance but the way of Life, and what is Life but God?

Dance is a sacred art form, and it is also catalytic in helping us to achieve altered states of consciousness through which we may perceive and interact with the Divine. The next time you find yourself surrounded by wild drummers and leaping flames, please remember that the Goddess is dancing, and she is calling to you.

Interview with Kirsty

Kirsty is the founder and artistic director of the Fringe Youth Dance Theatre in Toowoomba, Australia, an edgy, poignant, and highly contemporary group of passionate and invigorating dancers. Kirsty has been a high-school dance teacher for several years now. She describes herself as a "revolutionary with a fated life."

How did you come to dance? Has it always been an integral part of your life?

If I did not dance, I imagine I would feel emotionally void. I am generally perceived as an introverted person, so when dancing/choreographing, it's an opportunity for people to see a hint of "me." It's the only way I feel best expresses a part of my being that otherwise lies dormant. For most of us, dance is a form of expression; I don't see myself any different than this, except that instead of the "happiness" of dancing at a club on the weekend, I end up with a plethora of emotions that are channelled through movement.

How does dance define your life?
How do you, in turn, define dance?

Dance is what I know best. It seems to be the first and final thought of most days and encapsulates who I am. As cliché as it may seem, dance and I are inseparable; there is no way to tell where one begins and the other ends. The world of dance tends to be a consuming passion—most probably with many artistic and cultural pursuits. Being ultimately an expression of self, it is often difficult to define yourself without it. This can be a tragic circumstance at times, especially when I find myself hitting a low point artistically; there is no way to separate this moment from everyday life. However, I have never wanted for anything more. As a mother and artist, I find that I am more satisfied with life, and when practicing my art form, I feel most at home.

In your experience, can the act of dancing
free the spirit and move the body and mind
into different states of consciousness?

I definitely believe this is possible—for some people, that is. No doubt everyone feels good when dancing—natural endorphins are released through the body, as with a gym session, hiking through the great outdoors, or physical intimacy. However, freeing the spirit through movement requires not just a release through the physical but also the mental inhibitions that lock people down. Reflectively speaking, resonating beat clubs or drumming circles, the commonality of people around me, and the willingness to leave imperfection and question behind have always led to moments of liberation. The ability to free the spirit through dance is mostly accessible for those of us who quite simply engage in the moment. Like a surge of adrenalin, the beat and movement characteristically begin rhythmically and repetitively spiralling and surging upwards and outwards of the body, until we experience that undeniable state of ecstasy or happiness.

How do you approach dance? Are there any exercises or rituals you find helpful in focussing the body and the mind?

When I have the opportunity to focus on my body as a dancer, or if I am directing a class into a more inward and centred lesson, we begin with yoga sequences and Pilates stretches to focus on the breath of the body. It is an invaluable process of any lesson to make that connection between our breath and the body's movement. To further distinguish the core of movement and body, I perform the contemporary techniques of spinal rolls and floor rolls.[12] Both of these activities focus on grounding our body weight into the floor. The practices of breathing, centring, and grounding are the impetus for my movement practices, stimulating mind-body control as well as being beneficial for tuning the dancer's body.

What forms or styles of dance do you find are most effective with trance work, self-hypnosis, and the raising of power?

In dance, we characteristically identify ritual dance through several elements. To mention just a few: simple and repetitive movements, grounded circular patterning, arms raised upwards to the heavens, performing in a sacred place, symbolic gestures and costuming, drumming/bells, and human calls for aural accompaniment. Much in the same way as ritual dance is performed, I see trance work achieving its goal. In no way would the codified steps of ballet, the commercial and competitive nature of hip hop, or even the centred practices of contemporary dance

---

12 Spinal rolls and floor rolls are characteristic of modern contemporary dance styles. They are used especially to warm up the body of a dancer before routine work. Specifically, a spinal roll is the gradual, vertically aligned downwards roll of the spine as the dancer dips their head, neck, shoulders, and back to parallel the alignment of the legs. A floor roll can be any and all movements that use the floor/ground as the pivotal axis, or foundation. Floor rolls build balance, grace, and rhythm.

achieve this. Trance work is free from stylized movement. Its most common ally is ritual dance. I most often associate this work with the collective movement rituals at Woodford Folk Festival or the trance dancers in clubs or at doofs.[13] The movement elements have a commonality of grounded and repetitive footwork. There is an innate connectedness to the earth. The music and calls form the base of rhythm in the body. As the music builds and layers, so too does the rhythm in the body. We often find ourselves becoming more frenzied, our actions becoming more upright, elevating our body and hands towards the sky. And with this surge of adrenalin, which has been spiralling through the body looking for its exit point, it releases out. We hit that high point of ecstasy; we smile and simultaneously feel interconnected with everything around us.

When you dance, do you become someone or something else, or do you remain completely yourself, if not enhanced?

When dancing, in essence I remain myself. I embody a state of being rather than a character. This may take the form of a memory or emotion. This is what makes my experience and performance unique to me, my students, and my audience. Non-stylised movement is my most favoured form. When dancing at festivals, I best describe it as being the person I actually want to be—happy, free of inhibitions, and connected to the people around me.

---

13 "Doof" is Australian slang for a rave party, referring especially to the bass sound.

το τουch

Love is a verb.
—Unknown

Touch is a sacred art form. It too is an expression of the spirit within, channelled most often through raw passion and sensuality. In itself, touch is a neutral medium for expression—unless, like so many things, it is harnessed to either extreme. It is always important to be ethical and to integrate that wholly into your life.

In my life, the art of touch generally manifests either through my sexuality or the blessed massage (sometimes they meet). My friends and I are generally very candid with each other. We are unashamed of our sexuality, and our sexual experiences form a popular topic of discussion. The act of sex is a sacrament to my goddess Aphrodite (and to so many other love and sex deities) and to the Great Mother herself, who declares that "all acts of love and pleasure are my rituals." When I have sex and make love, I bless it as a prayer to Aphrodite. With every caress, a soaring syllable of my whispered prayer is sent to the Golden Goddess. This holy act can be reclaimed from the labels of "dirt" and "smut." I visualise making love as a pouring of the waters of one's grail into another's—sharing intimacy is the aim and the journey.

Touch is all-pervasive. It is often noted by many newcomers to Paganism that we Pagans love to hug—and nothing says "I acknowledge and honour the Divine within you" like a well-meant physical embrace. Once perfect trust is attained in a relationship, touch is a tried and true method of creating comfort between people. If applied correctly and with pure intent, touch can help to soothe an upset friend, open channels of communication, excite the senses, and bring healing and wholeness to the body.

I have had several truly intense experiences through sacred touch. One involved massaging a roommate in a share house I used to live in. She was leaning against my body as my legs flanked her torso. I centred and then channelled healing power into her as I massaged her shoulders, neck, arms, and back. After about five or ten minutes of this, we both simultaneously began to breathe raggedly and audibly as if we were having sex! This increased in intensity as my hands continued to work into her flesh, and then hot flushes, followed by cool, relieving sweats swept wave after wave through our bodies. It was as if our flesh had merged together, and the dance of this union had empowered our experience. Another experience that burns brightly in my mind was one of the last devotional circles I had in my garden temple at my mother's house, before I moved away from home after finishing school. I was meditating, and then suddenly I had the desire to dig a small hole in the soil with my fingers. The whole process felt very sensual to me, and I knew that on some level I was making love with the earth—a beautiful thing!

Pressure Touch

Pressure touch is a technique I learnt while learning contemporary dance in high school. My teacher gave no name to this method; however, I have passed on the technique several times now as "pressure touch," which describes it rather aptly.

You can practise pressure touch alone or with a partner (or several) and in larger company. In the ritual of land at the summation of this part of the book, I suggest it as the way to cast the circle. There are two principles of pressure touch, and with a bit of obviousness they are "pressure" and "touch." The individual places their palms on the partner's (or their own) body and applies a soft pressure, increasing gradually with time. The pressure should never be so intense that it arouses pain; it should only reach a firm level. In terms of where the pressure should be applied on the body, the answer is anywhere and everywhere. Be intuitive! In partner and group work, it is essential to always ascertain what boundaries (if any) there are when it comes to physical touch.

Ground and centre; breathing deeply, begin to channel energy through your flexed palms, and then place them on either your own skin or someone else's and gradually increase pressure. This is also a useful way to revitalise the body and to cast spells: simply hold strong a particular intent while performing pressure touch. Once again, as with any touch, this technique can border on the sensual and can easily become it if the participants are open to it. Exercise with ethics always.

4

TO DIVINE THE LAND

*Nature is the physical reality of spirit. It is not separate from
the human spirit. Seeking a greater truth than the physical
world reveals, you have entered this natural flow.*
—Michael J. Roads, *Journey into Nature*

The land itself is Spirit incarnate. It is a manifestation of the Divine
right before our eyes and under our feet. We can connect and work
with the land directly because as physical beings, it is a simple and
nourishing act to delve into our environmental surroundings. As all
is connected in a great web of life, we are able to access anything we
can possibly imagine. We can find meaning through the beauty of
synchronicity and discover omens and portents in the natural world,
because it is in the middleworld in which the Divine expresses through
the medium of what is apparent and what can be sensed with our
innate animal instincts. The land is a wisdom keeper of secrets, which
can be discovered through the right channels. The efficacy of these
channels depends, of course, on the preparedness and state of consciousness of the individual who is doing the divining.

Many ancient indigenous traditions teach ways and methods of omen interpretation. These omens, signs, and portents, products of a world of synchronicity, can be found in the landscape just as much as they can be glimpsed in the heavens or seen in the tarot or the runes. One such example can be found in Ross Heaven's brilliant account of his tutelage under one of the last remaining Welsh sin eaters in the Celtic healing traditions—*The Sin Eater's Last Confessions* (Llewellyn, 2008).

In Heaven's book, he speaks of Adam, his Welsh sin-eating teacher, guiding him in a practical exercise called *rhamanta* in his wisdom tradition. Ross is directed to intuitively find three places in which he is to close his eyes, hold a question in mind, spin around three times, open his eyes, and mark the first sight as an omen. This process is repeated three times (once for every place), and the three omens are then woven together to create a story—a divinatory pattern, or theme. As Adam says, "Dream yourself into this story, and see what it tells you about your life."

OMENWALKING

Nature, you see, is the visible face of spirit and will reveal the truth to us. All we need do is listen and have faith in what we are told.
—Ross Heaven, *The Sin Eater's Last Confessions* (Adam's words)

Most of us take walks. However, a walk with a purpose is something not everyone has considered. In many indigenous societies, there are various spiritual pilgrimages that can aid the individual in discerning one's fate, purpose, or truth/s. In many Native American cultures, these pilgrimages are sometimes called vision quests. Omenwalking is another interpretation of the concept.

Taking an omenwalk is as simple as clearing the mind, focussing on a question/goal/purpose, and then taking a walk! Open yourself to the influence of fate/divinity and move around the world in keen consciousness; however, it doesn't pay to be *too* alert. Move as if through honey or in a dream, and cultivate an attitude of innocence and wonder. Take note of everything you see and feel on your walk. Once you feel you have your answers, or at least have gained some understanding, gratefully return home (or continue the walk) and reflect on the experience. Just as with the sin eater's technique, look for the patterns joining each "discrete" thing, and a story will unfold.

To ground this technique in reality, I will provide a personal experience. When I lived with my mother and sister in Toowoomba, I used to go on regular walks to the local Japanese gardens. It was one of my sacred spaces—a power place. I took a walk one Ostara to bathe in the blessed newness that is spring. As I journeyed, a breeze sailed through a jacaranda tree and sent all the purple blossoms fluttering through the air—I showered in the cascade and relished it! Upon entering the gardens, I received a call from a friend of mine; we spoke about a big party that we were attending that night. Not a moment after she rang, I stumbled into a bush beside a stream in which two geese were guarding their nest of eggs; it was one of the most beautiful sights I had ever seen. Despite the absolute appropriateness of my experience on the day of the spring equinox, my "pilgrimage" meant a lot to me, as I had felt for some time that I was coming to a rebirth. The shower of jacaranda blossoms felt like a cleansing, and seeing the eggs (the potential for new life) confirmed my feelings.

CAIRNS AND LABYRINThS

Divining the land isn't only about receiving answers through the omens, signs, and wisdom of nature; Paganism is a spirituality of sacred exchange. We receive manifold gifts from the Divine, and so we give back to honour what is given so freely.

Many Pagans enjoy capturing, channeling, and enhancing the natural flow of the life force that runs through the land by creating specific physical alignments to do the job. In megalithic times, the various tribal people of Europe did just that—with stones. Similarly, many ancient shrines, temples, and altars are built on sites where lines of power (variously called ley lines, dragon lines, or song lines) intersect. This principle of the intersection of lines, or paths, also surfaces in the folkloric belief that crossroads are potent places for magickal workings.

When I was travelling through the British Isles, my friends and I were lucky enough to happen upon Castlerigg Stone Circle in Cumbria, England. This understated megalithic monument is cradled in a picturesque Cumbrian valley and surrounded by beautiful blue mountains. While at the circle, I began to walk widdershins subconsciously, but by the end of the full circuit I realised I had released quite a weight! I also had time to speak with some of the stones. I asked one stone rather straightforwardly why it was placed there to begin with. The stone's answer was curt and matter-of-fact: "To channel power, of course!" How could I forget?

Below, you will find a ritual of consecration for the creation and devotion of a cairn. A cairn is simply a pile of stones that have been placed with clear intent and purpose, often fulfilling the function of a shrine, or spirit house. I have built cairns several times before, and I find the process to be highly meditative. It has even been suggested to me that cairn building can be a great way to cast spells; simply think about the desired outcome as you build, charge, and dedicate your cairn. If you decide to construct a labyrinth instead, you only need to create the labyrinth pattern with a viable boundary marker—this could be eco-friendly paint on grass, spaced-out candles, or perhaps, if you felt up to it, you could make and mark cairns as the boundaries. The same ritual of consecration can be applied to a labyrinth—merely prolong the meditation for the entirety of the labyrinth making, and then bless, charge, and consecrate with the elements.

A Ritual of Consecration for the Creation and Devotion of a Cairn

You will need:

- Frankincense, sage, or sandalwood stick incense (for air)
- One white taper candle (for fire)
- Jasmine or rose essential oil (for water)
- Flowers (for earth)
- Stones (various sizes, similar shape; flat and oblong work marvellously!)

Ground and centre. Gather the stones around you, and begin to build the cairn. Remember to place the sturdier, flatter, and larger stones at the bottom to create a strong foundation. Generally, cairns are tapered and somewhat hollow structures; however, in this case, make sure you leave enough space in the centre for a candle to fit nicely and for your hand to fit through to secure it.[14] As you build the cairn, enter a meditative state, and with each placing of a new stone, think about or feel a different quality or emotion to imbue your offering to the Divine with potency and magick. If you like, you could even write down a list of words beforehand that you could say aloud during the building process.

After the cairn is physically complete, you may bless, charge, and consecrate it with the power and aid of the elements. Firstly, insert the candle into the space inside the cairn and light it, praying to the spirit/s of fire and calling forth its gifts. Approach each element in turn as you light the incense and smudge the cairn for

---

14 When it comes to outdoor ritual work and candles, fire safety always needs to be taken into consideration. Either remain with the candle until it burns out completely or snuff out the candle when you are finished with the ritual or working; you may like to return at a later date to light it again. Never leave a fire unattended, no matter how small.

air, anoint the cairn with the essential oil for water, and adorn it with flowers for earth. Hold your hands over the cairn and direct and channel power into it to animate it. When you feel ready, proclaim the cairn blessed, charged, and consecrated! If you like, you can chant my tradition's blessing chant as you pour energy into the cairn:

I bless, I cleanse, I consecrate, I purify, I charge!

5

RITUAL

This ritual can be celebrated either as a solitary or with a group. It is a Neopagan ritual with Celtic, Wiccan, and Witchcraft influences, and this will be the general trend of most rituals presented within this book.

You will need:

- One white taper candle
- Incense made up of 3 drops of patchouli essential oil, 1 part copal, and 2 parts frankincense resin
- Brazier and charcoal disc
- Natural offerings (e.g., flowers or food)

The land ritual will work best if it is carried out beneath a tree.[15] You can choose to set up an altar, but in this case, simplicity is key.

---

15 If possible, all three rituals (for land, for sky, and for sea) should be carried out under the same tree. The tree will act as a physical reinforcement of the shamanic reality of the world tree.

Ground and Centre

Ground and centre using the tree of life alignment meditation. Now, in this calm and centred state, verbally acknowledge the indigenous guardians and spirits of the place and ask for their blessings on the ritual. Now it is time to form the space (to cast the circle).

Cast the Circle

The circle will be cast through sacred pressure touch. If alone, place pressure on the ground at the four directions and visualise the circle forming as you go. If in a group, it is better to form a physical chain and for each person to touch the person next to them in a deosil manner. The person in the east will begin, and then, going deosil, the touch will continue until a physical chain is created and everyone is linked through sacred touch. Each person should speak one line of the following chant as they touch the neighbouring person:

> By the land,
> By the Mother
> By my body...

The chant should continue for a minute or two, with everyone chanting together. At the right time, the circle should be affirmed:

> The circle is cast. I/We are now between the
> worlds, in all the worlds. So mote it be.

Acknowledge Land, Sky & Sea

If alone, make all three gestures independently while mentally or verbally acknowledging the corresponding realm. In a group situation, appoint three different people to a respective realm (one for land, one for sky, and one for sea). The gestures/words for each realm are as follows:

Land: Place both hands on the ground—*"By the land…"*

Sky: Hold hands open and up to the sky—*"By the sky…"*

Sea: Cup both hands together in front of the navel—*"And by the sea…"*

All together, say, *"By the ancient trinity, so mote it be!"*

To seal the blessing, trace a triquetra (♉) in the air with the first two fingers of your power/dominant hand.

Place a candle at the foot of the tree; it is lit to represent the fire of the Divine, where the three realms are one.

Blessing of the Land

Now is the time to place your offerings at the foot of the tree. As you do, affirm your dedication and devotion to the Mother who is our nourishing earth and vow to always defend her and uphold her health and well-being, as we are all one in the Mother.

If you are celebrating this ritual with a group, you may stand (or appoint someone else) as challenger, and recite the following charge to inspire before the offerings are placed:

My sisters and brothers in the land, I bless you in the name of the Great Mother, who holds within herself all life. Like the first flower of spring and the ready stalk of grain, you are nurtured by the land. I pray that, in return, you will nurture and care for the land, our Mother. If this is your most sacred will, this is the time to make it known. Place your offering in the name of the Goddess and speak aloud your promise.

Guided Land Meditation

You are standing at the foot of an emerald green hill that rises in the centre of a valley surrounded by wild forest. You notice that the trees seem to be spiralling through the seasons timelessly. First you see the vivid greens of summer, then the red, orange, and yellow leaves fall from the branches and leave them bare and skeletal. Just as quickly and seamlessly, however, the flourish of green returns, and the trees blossom with life. You sigh and find that your heart beats in rhythm with the beelike hum rising from the land.

You find yourself suddenly attracted to the crest of the hill, though you feel the weaving of fate as you begin the climb. On the top of the hill stands an ancient menhir, a standing stone, and a pale woman in a flowing forest green dress guards it. Her shining red hair is twisted into a pattern of braids, almost like Celtic knotwork, and her hands rest on her pregnant belly. She smiles at you as you approach the standing stone, and you kneel and bow your head to her, for you realise who she is: the sovereignty of the land. When you look up, she has disappeared, and you discover an indentation in the stone, which you can comfortably sit in. You sit down and survey the valley, which turns into forests…mountains…plains…desert…rainforest…bushland…

You are now in a different place altogether. You can feel the sun beating down on your hardened skin, and you can see heat shimmering on the horizon. You are standing in a red desert plain, but you look to your right and see a rushing river. The black-silted banks are lined with eucalyptus and gum trees, and the air has a sharp fragrance to it. In the distance you can see a vast red earth mound, and just as you begin to ponder what this mound could be, you find yourself standing right next to it.

A black woman smiles down at you from the top of the earth mound, and wordlessly she summons a song of power. You feel it thrumming through the air, and you feel encouraged to climb up the mound to the woman. She gestures to you, smiling, giving you permission.

You reach her and once more kneel and bow, but when you look up, there she remains. You realise now that this woman too holds her pregnant belly and shines with light. You find yourself lost in her deep eyes, and in their depths you see women. Each woman is differently shaped and sized and in every colour of the rainbow. Then you begin to see men emerging in the vision, and then trees, plants, and animals. Rejoicing in this vision, you silently shout your gratitude to the universe.

In that moment, you find that your vision disappears, and all you see now are stars. Perhaps you also see the white moon and the radiant, blazing sun. You feel at one with all of this, and then slowly it dawns upon you that you are the planet Earth herself looking up at the glory of the cosmos. You feel weightlessly grounded and so at peace with yourself and your surroundings. You feel strong, and you are aware of every tendril and current of vitality that streams through your vast, deep blue/green/black/red body. You are the land, and you realise now that all that dwell with and on the land are a part of it. Blessed be.

Raise and Release the Power

To raise the power in this ritual, you will be stamping the solid earth with your feet in time with the rhythm of the piece of land you are celebrating on. As you do this, focus on the health, well-being, and protection of our Mother Earth and all that is within and a part of her holy biosphere. You may chant the following if you feel the need for words to guide you:

Deep below we/I call ye up
Power of earth, raise the power,
Twist and turn and fuel our/my spell
In this time and in this hour.

When it is time to release the power, make it known to the others (if in a group) and throw your arms into the air, directing and channeling the flow of power back into the earth. Know that your work is blessed and sealed with intent and purity of heart.

Open the Space

Snuff out the candle flame and acknowledge the blessings of the three realms, the world tree that joins them, and the indigenous guardians and spirits of place. Open the circle by moving widdershins and visualising the sphere of light dispersing into the air and the earth. Do this in silence, as this can help to ground the excess energy your body may retain after magickally intensive work. Leave the offerings beneath the tree, and eat and drink something to further ground your body.

SKY

PART
TWO

CORRESPONDENCES

Classical Element	Air
Shamanic World	Upperworld
Themes	Clarity, communication, enlightenment, expansion, foresight (sacred sight), knowing, the realm of the gods, transcendence, vision, wisdom
Cultural/Esoteric Symbols	Angels (angelic beings), the athame/wand of the Craft tools, birds (of prey), the blue sky, clouds/rain/storms, the moon, pillars, stars, the sun, the sword of the gifts of the Tuatha De Danann, upright triangle/pyramids
Herbs/Plants	Acacia, almond, benzoin, bergamot, bodhi, broom, caraway, dandelion, eyebright, fenugreek, goldenrod, hazel, jasmine, lavender, lemongrass, lemon verbena, meadowsweet, mistletoe, myrrh, oak, palm, sage, slippery elm
Colours	Azure/sky blue, black, gold, grey, silver, white, yellow

6

TO TRANSCEND
AND EXPAND

I am a child of earth and starry heaven, of this I know...
—Orphic tablet

The sky is the realm of transcendence, at least from the land-dwelling perspective. It is above and beyond, and therefore it is a symbol of the mystery of the gods. In shamanic journeying, the road through and to the worlds is, of course, the world tree (the cosmic highway). To ascend to the sky realm, one must scale the tree and find wings of one's own or persuade the great bird perching in the topmost branches to act as an astral mount. This great bird is described variously as an eagle, the magickal Muan bird of the Mayans, or the Garuda of Hindu mythology.

The star-strung indigo nations are the home of ageless wisdom, and indeed there are many theories as to whether we ourselves descend from a race of super beings who came from a faraway planet or galaxy. Other ideas are based on the belief in alien visitation or that we are the workers of gods, who oversee their paradise. I personally attach no particular value or belief to any of these theories, though

I have a few intuitions regarding similar things. What I would like to illustrate here, however, is the ancient teaching of cosmic "out there" origins. One of the unearthed Orphic[16] tablets was translated to reveal a statement or magickal/initiatory response that expresses the belief that we as humans, and perhaps all of life on earth, are children of this planet and the heavens. We contain within our beings the same "stuff" that was there with the Big Bang. Therefore, it is in our nature to seek out the solace of the sky, just as we are nourished and supported by the land, our earth.

In this chapter, I will outline magickal methods to aid in transcendence and expansion. They will largely consist of mental work, with an aim of becoming all-encompassing. The techniques below will require a sound psychological state, a peaceful being, and a receptive mind. This magick of transcendence and expansion will take you out of your head and into the celestial realms of ether and light. You have celebrated your body, and now you will explore the limitless potential of your mind's ability to soar.

TO RECEIVE GNOSIS

Thou art Goddess; Thou art God.
—Church of All Worlds saying

In my book *Spirited,* I offer the reader a Gnostic exercise on page 149. *Gnosis* is ancient Greek for "knowledge" and refers here to the attainment of divine knowledge and understanding.

---

16 The Orphics were an ancient Greek mystery cult whose mythos, cosmology, and practices were said to be inspired by the mytho-historical figure of Orpheos. Orpheos descended into the underworld to win his wife, Eurydike, back from Persephone and Hades by playing his sweet music to them. They were so moved by his music that they agreed to return Eurydike to Orpheos under one condition: that he not look back at her until they had returned to the land of the living. Orpheos broke this promise and thus condemned his wife to an eternity with the dead. This shamanic journey of sacrifice for greater wisdom inspired the Orphics to view the realities of the kosmos (cosmos—the world) in a different vein to the state cultus of the time, and thus they formed a society unto themselves.

The early Gnostic Christian sects had an implicit belief in duality. They believed that matter was a product of the Demiurge (the fallen spirit descended from Sophia, the Divine Feminine), and that if one could ascend through the spheres, one could be rid of matter, the earth, and the physical, and be at home once more with the true God (from whom we originated). The core of any Gnostic tradition, however, is not the duality of flesh versus spirit but the idea that we each contain a spark of the Divine within that is eternally connected to its source, which many identify as "God."

In the Pagan traditions, we are taught to be aware of our divine natures. This is reflected once more through the Orphic teachings and the modern Church of All Worlds affirmation of divinity quoted on the facing page. The depth of connectivity between all things forms the basis of the practice of magick and the experience of immanent divinity. The Divine is both here and there; it is the land, and it is the mystery of the heavens. To transcend the linearity and routine of mundane life is to cease to be an automaton and to awaken true consciousness—to seek the knowledge of the cosmos. When we expand our awareness to encompass more than what we are offered by society, we become vessels for gnosis.

This gnosis has been expressed in many ways in the diverse cultures of the earth throughout history:

In Lak'ech (Mayan)—I am another you.

Namaste (modern Hindi and Sanskrit)—I bow to the Divine in you.

Thou art God/dess (Church of All Worlds)—You are the Divine, wholly in yourself.

Ultimately, it is about becoming aware of the bigger picture that we ourselves are unique embodiments of; each and every one of us is a perfect expression of the great mystery of life. I am the microcosm to the macrocosm. Much of my work in this life so far has been to delve deeply into my being and ignite and bring blazing passion to the fire that burns at the core of me and of us all. This incandescent flame is what connects us with the great ring of fire that is creation, destruction, purification, and making anew. This is the ring of fire I have seen Shiva and Dionysos dance in and through. It is the transformation of reality—its eternal mutability. Change is the law. To attain gnosis is to surrender, release ego, and be free. In freedom we discover rhythm, and therein lies the magick of the world. For Pagans, this is a powerful pathway to true enlightenment. Once we learn to let go and let the gods, we have learnt the art of life, and not just the joy of it. The art cultivates the joy, bringing finer enrichment. Knowledge is also power, and power leads to greater potency in experience, circumstance, and truth. It is through the power of knowing that we become all-encompassing, transcendent beings of the sky. This realm of sky imbues us with the gifts of foresight, intuition, clarity, understanding, and wisdom. The following techniques will aid in developing gnosis in your life.

TO LET GO

To let go is the first step in achieving gnosis. Firstly, we must release our human attachment to the persona and identity that we create to stabilise and comfort the wilder aspects of our deeper mysteries. In letting go, we allow peace to reign completely in our lives, for in releasing the ego and the socially propounded idea that the external and foreign is chaotic in the destructive, self-erasing sense, we learn to accept the being that, in truth, flows with the continuum that is harmony within and of itself.

Harmony, equilibrium, and balance underlie the life force that is the current of the world. The pure will of nature—of the Divine, of the gods—knows itself wholly and seeks only to flow in harmony with itself. This does not produce a stasis in which change is denied, it is merely an observation of nature's tendency to perpetuate itself, and through death and transformation to enliven and empower its unique and diverse expressions.

If we let go, we too realise the pure will that we are so much a part of, and we are initiated—we become vessels for the power that is generated by the flow of the continuum!

Relax into yourself and centre through deep rhythmic breathing. Release the tension in your body, and allow your body and spirit to move as they choose to, or be still. If you begin to sway, embrace the sway and let it be until it plays out of its own accord. Consciously ignite every cell within your body. Feel each cell flare and then dim once more. Breathe with every pore of your skin and soak in the power of the world. At the same time, give back what you take in, and let it cycle over and over in this way. Now, in this moment, release… let it all go…simply be.

TO BE FREE

Once we attain being (because we have let go), we begin to flow with the currents of awakening. We awaken to the truth of freedom—that we *are* free! The Charge of the Goddess, that most famous Wiccan declaration, states explicitly that freedom is a principle of life that should be held in high esteem. In fact, it should be practised actively, and being skyclad in ritual is suggested as a sign of freedom. I would have to agree that nudity is something that does make me feel free, as it is a state that I am only ever in for about an hour each day. In the summer months, however, I enjoy sleeping naked, and when opportunity knocks and I find myself in the wilderness near a body of water (or under the cloak of night), I enjoy throwing myself clothes-free into the cool embrace of the liquid realms.

Being free should go hand in hand with knowing we are free. In fact, the knowledge of personal freedom should then lead to one's embracing of it. The journey to freedom begins with the self. The

self, the you that is you, needs to accept this primal truth wholeheartedly—that we are already free—before true freedom is felt. True freedom is knowing that you are here, now, breathing and alive and divine
because of it! What more could someone need to realise freedom?

> *You are now flowing with, and as the pure will of, nature. You are*
> *the continuum. You are peace and balance between all things. One-*
> *ness pervades you. You are liberated from isolation, and yet you feel*
> *the you that is you; you also know the you that is you is the we that*
> *is we, and the whole that is whole. Colourful lights of Faerie spin*
> *seductively around you as you flow through All! You taste, you smell,*
> *you touch, you hear and see. Every sense is beyond itself, and you spi-*
> *ral into implosion, only to ricochet back and forth in mirthful aban-*
> *don from one corner of the universe to the next. You are delight and*
> *ecstasy, and you are truly free!*

TO KNOW

Freedom leads to the will and desire to know. The knowledge I am
speaking of does not seek to condense or constrain a reality or a truth
with conceptualisation or symbology. This gnosis, or knowledge,
grants the seeker a further gift of freedom and letting go. It is as if a
tyrannical oppressor suddenly became a saint and released his slaves.
They leave the stronghold of grey timelessness and journey out into
the world with relief because they have been freed, and through journeying and dancing, they truly realise it. Then the former "master"
invites the ex-slaves back for a revel! With suspense and hearts titil-
lated by apprehension, the people come and smile at the radiant saint,
who they could never compare with the cruel tyrant that had once
robbed them of all liberty. The saint holds up a mirror, and you see
yourself in the reflection. You too are a shining saint, and you had
never truly lost anything; you only thought you had!

Then the words that soothe all wounds are spoken. If spoken with meaning and true understanding, they are the mightiest healer and the sovereignty of all. Together, holding hands, breathing the same breath, hearts beating as one: "I love you." The reverberations of this intonation of divinity sets forth wave after wave of more love, for love begets more love, and through freedom we accept in our hearts what we have always known—that love is creator, continuum, and created. Love is knowing that the Divine birthed us, and we will birth the Divine. We are walking not in the shadows of the gods but in their footsteps. Gnosis has ignited upon the brow of the seeker! Gnosis has initiated again!

Breathe, release, be free, know—heart beating, body sighing—feel truth; let it be—in this moment, in all moments—you are Divine... forever.

7

TO WEAVE WITH MAGICK

Witches embrace positive change, and when this change
does not occur spontaneously, they create it.
—Janet Farrar & Gavin Bone, *Progressive Witchcraft*

The quantum realities that are being explored by cutting-edge scientists currently speak of the unity of things that Witches, shamans, and mystics have known for millennia. Having no beyond-the-surface understanding of quantum theory myself, at least in the scientific sense, I will not embellish further on that field here. What I feel inclined to provide in this chapter is a methodology of working and weaving with that subtle metaphor (and reality) of energy that will not only enhance your skills in this area but align you with the life force so that you are in constant conscious connection with it. Like gnosis, this depth of acceptance, understanding, and being will not only empower you in every sense but will gift you with that ethereal (and yet so earthly) grace that has always been a side effect of the lives we live and the work we do.

THE WYRD

*Like a spider's web, the web of wyrd is fragile yet
sturdy…so delicately balanced that the gentlest
tug transmits along all of its threads.*
—Freya Aswynn, *Northern Mysteries & Magick*

Weaving with magick is a charge within itself. The basic premise of Witchcraft is that all is interconnected and thus we are each intimately connected to everything else. We are empowered to consciously effect change and transformation within the web that is the energetic blueprint of this underlying reality. How one goes about this determines the character, or "colour," of the individual's intent, and intent is the driving force of magickal work. However, a debate on foundational ethics will not be embarked on in this book.[17]

The web that I speak of has been called many things, but it is the Anglo-Saxon concept and theme of "Wyrd" that speaks the message and truth of what enlivens and empowers Witches to weave as we do.

The Wyrd can't be explained easily. It is one of those things that, even as a writer and a Witch, I cannot aptly or with justice describe. I could dance, sing, and make love, and yet though each of those things would express the Wyrd, the Wyrd is too big for one creative outlet to allow it singular expression.

The Wyrd is that thing which is everything. It is vibration; it is cause and effect; it is the foundational laws that created the metaphor and energy exchange of cause and effect (and what binds together the continuum of flow) in the first place.[18] Wyrd is fate, and it is not predestined. It is spiralling and it is dissolving. It is oneness and it is plurality. It is the paradox and the great mystery, and yet it is just a

---

17 See my book *Spirited: Taking Paganism Beyond the Circle* for an entire chapter devoted to Pagan ethics.

18 Though nothing happens in isolation; spirals, cycles, connectivity—these are the ways of nature and the cosmos.

web. The beauty of Wyrd is that the less you say, the more you say, and that is a beautiful thing. Now, an interjection…

One rainy day, two Witches heard a knock at their door. There, standing awkwardly, however nicely dressed, were two delightful Jehovah's Witnesses. Arione, the Freisian Witch, invited the two bedraggled Witnesses in for tea. Over the next hour or so, the Witches and the Witnesses spoke of many things—work, travel, the beautiful home they sat drinking tea in, and finally, of course, religion! The four discussed many aspects of spirituality, and everyone seemed decidedly passionate about the subject. Of course, one cannot discuss religion and spirituality without mentioning the Divine!

"We find it strange and overtly patriarchal that the Divine is only referred to as a 'he' in the Bible," said the Balinese-Celtic Witch.

"I'm all for women!" declared the female Witness. "But I believe the Bible refers to God as male because it is easy for the world to relate to a loving father."

The two Witches exchanged a perturbed glance.

"And what of the Mother—where we all, as humans, were birthed from? The woman who nourished us with milk and carried us for nine months as we grew and developed in the womb? This is a universal human experience. Where has the Mother gone? Is she obsolete?"

The two Witnesses seemed at a loss for words.

"The Divine is mystery—the great mystery is what we sometimes call it. It is life, it is spiralling wonder, it is in and out, it is everywhere, in everything, and possibly nowhere…what an expansive thing, the mystery. It's the thing we dance to, make love with, sing for, and eat. It's magickal," said the Witches, sighing because they felt and experienced this great mystery in every moment.

"Are you satisfied with a mystery, however? What if you could really know God?" piped a Witness.

The Witches smiled.

"We are totally satisfied—completely fulfilled and overflowing with ecstasy—a little drunk even. All this because the Divine, to us, is a mystery. And we know it deeply in our hearts."

The best way to experience the Wyrd is to do just that. Only you can determine how you will do so. Knowing Wyrd is almost a side effect of the other magickal work that we do. By casting a spell and seeing it come into fruition, I become aware of the Wyrd. By attaining gnosis and liberating my spirit, I gain the right consciousness to perceive the Wyrd's all-encompassing grandeur. By merrily sipping tea on a Wednesday afternoon in the company of Witnesses, I realise, "My oh my! This tea is good!" These are the gifts of the Wyrd, and through them we know it.

It is essential, at least, to be aware of the Wyrd when weaving with magick because one is of the other and the latter stems from the former. The Wyrd is not the originator of things, however; it is the "isness" of things. Magick, as my friend Awen said to me one day, is that "thatness" that is. In a worldview that experiences life as continuum versus a "start-finish" scenario, there is no reason to suggest (or need) a cause or originator of things.

In the WildWood Tradition of Witchcraft, of which I am an initiated priest, we acknowledge, honour, and celebrate the Weaver whose charge is the Wyrd. They are the two sides of the same coin. We call her first (out of our Sacred Four[19]) at our coven rituals. Our reasoning/feeling for this is that she, being of and residing with the Wyrd,

---

19 In the WildWood Tradition, we acknowledge, honour, and celebrate the Sacred Four, and this is comprised of the Weaver, the Green Man, the Crescent-Crowned Goddess, and the Stag-Horned God. We also acknowledge them in that order—for no particular reason; it merely developed naturally that way. The latter two have secret oathbound names that only members of the inner court know. This engenders intimacy and true initiatory experience. We are, technically speaking, hard polytheists, and thus we experience our gods as independent entities unto themselves, just as we are all complete within ourselves but undeniably and irrevocably interwoven and enmeshed within the whole mystery—as are the gods.

is our most primal foundation. We couldn't possibly do what we do or be what we are without this vibrating web of wonder. Remember that it is mystery, and when you know, you know. A wise Witness once observed, "You both seem so very fulfilled in your spirituality. That's amazing! I guess it's time to go. Thank you for the tea."

I imagine the Weaver likes to drink tea with the Wyrd…or perhaps the Wyrd is the tea and she is the cup.

Note: Having said all of the above, one of the best books I have ever read is actually about the Wyrd and is called *The Way of the Wyrd* by Brian Bates. I urge you to read it.

PAYING HOMAGE TO THE WEAVER

A close friend of mine (also a WildWood priestess) often says that the Weaver's gift is retrospect. Another friend mentioned to me that one becomes aware of the Wyrd in hindsight. The Weaver, the Wyrd, and the web are all words for the same concept—the underlying, radiant interconnectedness of things; fate singing in the veins of the All! The Weaver is that hugeness of life but also the smallest, most obscure detail. We call her Grandmother of Time, the Sovereign of Space, and the Silver-Bright Lady of Midnight Hour. When exploring the Wyrd and the web and the "bigger picture," it's a good idea to honour and pay homage to the Mother of it all. What follows is a devotional to the Weaver. Adapt it to suit your tastes/tradition/inclinations.

Stand before your altar or in a sacred space, and ground and centre. Align with the oneness of things, and kneel, bowing your head. Visualise and feel an expanse of nothingness—a void—in your mind, and be at peace with non-being until gradually you feel the subtle throbbing of a pulse—a pulse which is you, not you, and everything else. The pulse is the Weaver moving you to be and to exist. You smile, and a laugh all but bursts from your lips as you relish *being*! You feel her silver threads in everything you are, and you are proud and honoured to be her child. You hear a faint laughter that rings through the stardust and the swirling molecules of fate. Aloud, you say this prayer:

Silver-Bright Lady of Midnight Hour, Sovereign of Space, and Grandmother of Time, unto you am I. May I be in your arms, and by your laughter may I be. For you are the inspiration for the reason, just as you are the feeling in all things! I am a child of earth and starry heaven; in your name do I pray. Blessed be.

MOVING INTO, MOVING THROUGH

My soul, do not seek eternal life,
but exhaust the realm of the possible.
—Pindar, ancient Greek poet (Pythian III)

The expansion of consciousness is paramount to magickal work, which seeks to externalise the persona, free the spirit (journey-work), and bridge the gap between individuated perception and holistic worldviews (clear-seeing, or clairvoyance). Before one can attain aptitude at astral travel, the "sight," and other intuitive faculties, it is necessary to recognise, acknowledge, and celebrate the truth of non-separation—the fundamental principle of quantum reality. In understanding this universal truth of interconnection and interrelation (the Web of Wyrd), we find quintessence and realise the microcosm to the macrocosm—the self to the Self. This is moving into the centre. This centre is in all places, in all times; it is the initiator, the seed, the outcome, and the flow of the continuum of life. Moving through the centre is the perpetual, never-ending course and journey through the continuum of life. In fact, moving through is dancing the continuum.

If we are to centre ourselves in the continuum and then dance through it, we are in fact expanding our consciousness, liberating the spirit, and discovering the infinity of existence itself.

An Exercise in
Expanding Consciousness

Begin by deepening and prolonging your breath, and being only aware of the inhalation and the exhalation of air into, through, and out of your body. Continue with this rhythm until you reach the void. In that void, suspended in no-thing, vibrating silently, you feel wave after wave of palpable, throbbing "existence." As formless nothingness, a yearning begins to develop in the centre of something that feels distinctly unique to "you." The yearning is to go outward with the waves that pulse in the centre, and go forth into the surrounding darkness. In the far distance, each wave curls into itself, incandescent flashes of what looks like light flare, and you desire to be showered in that luminous glow so that you may see yourself and what you have become. You know inwardly that you are life seeking and yearning to know itself. You surf out with the next wave, and the exhilaration of the speed and the direct clarity of the aim fills you with ecstasy and propels your awareness into light. Showered in light, you find that you are now a star shining in a galaxy. As a star, you birth a solar system; through gravity, you draw to you cold space mass, and it forms into gaseous orbs of brilliant colours, and they orbit around you. In a moment, this is all forgotten, and you are a human being on a planet of flourishing and evolving life. It is a green and blue planet, and you thrive here. You find yourself on a vast plain; you crouch down to dig your hands into the dirt. As you do, the coolness of the soil reacts with your skin, and you fall into the dark womb of the Mother, who nourishes and sustains you. Deep down, in the centre of the earth, is her molten core—a star! You are light again! You rush outward, and in one explosive sigh of utter joy, your awareness expands to encompass all the planets, all the stars, all the galaxies, and all the worlds. You feel that there are so many sighs, and your sigh, in this infinitesimal moment, has synchronised with the others to create harmony, balance, and clarity. You know that the "edges" of your expanded consciousness are boundless, and you feel no end to your soaring, sighing truth of existence. For now, you are everywhere, in everything. You remember the origin of depth inside—the no-thing of no-where; the void of nonexistence that sought to see itself in the mirror. You are a child of that void, and you are a creator of the All which is life.

SIMPLE AND EFFECTIVE ENERGY WORK

I find that because energy is such an ambiguous concept, the work we do with energy can be just as vague and often misleading in terms of instructions. However, it is essential for a Witch to have a good energetic grounding because this is fundamental to our Craft. Energy is what we weave with; it is what we raise, channel, direct, and release when we are engaging magickally with the world. Indeed, in my mind, it should be compulsory learning at schools! However, I digress.

In an aspirant training session with my coven in early 2009, I asked each of the Witches present what they felt energy is. I smiled (verging on laughter) as they, one to the other, came up with more definitions for energy than the number of people in the room. This is the point. Energy *is* electrical charge; it *is* interaction and interface between living things; it *is* transformation, change, and catalyst; and it definitely *is* life force. It is also a creative metaphoric expression for all these things, because essentially the concept of "energy" is meaningless. Energy is not necessarily a substance or a current of force—but it is very real and present within all things. It is what qualifies our experiences. Energy is life. To me, energy is synonymous with magick.

To further your relationship with magickal energy, I have provided an arsenal of energetic exercises below for the avid Witch. I have also provided a very brief introduction on quantum physics so that you may ground your magick in "scientific" understandings. It is always good to know that science is validating our experiences out there in the "real" world, but never let it justify who you are, or make or break your trust in how you experience life. Like everything, balance is the key.

EXPLORING QUANTUM 101

The new physics revealed to us that a complete understanding of reality requires more than the capabilities of rational thought.
—Reginald Crosley, M.D., *The Vodou Quantum Leap*

Quantum physics and the reality (or the lack thereof, perhaps) it postulates is often touted as one of the greatest scientific validations of magick, Witchcraft, and all things generally deemed "supernatural." Whether or not Witches and other magickal folk need this validation can be argued, as I for one do not require it for my spiritual "security." However, it is often helpful when sharing dialogue with individuals who do not engage in magickal / spiritual things to be able to ground a common understanding of our cosmologies, philosophies, and sacred truths with what modern society likes to call science.

The basic premise of quantum physics is that beneath, behind, and underlying absolutely everything is a reality that animates and charges all things to appear to exist. This "subatomic façade," as I have called it, weaves itself in dynamic fashion (of course!) through what quantum physicists like to call waves and particles. However, the catch is that while much of "energy" is predisposed to the wave dynamic / quality, there are finite points of "reality" that can be pinpointed as particles. These particles disappear and reappear simultaneously at "opposite" ends of the universe without travelling the distance between, and there have been several experiments that have captured and observed this phenomenon. The key here is that the observer affects the observed—our "reality" is observer dependent. Nothing can be measured until the moment we choose to take measure. In a nutshell, we have an effect over the universe simply through the active awareness of our perception, or consciousness.

Starhawk often speaks of all life forms as beings of consciousness that swirl and become one with the sea of consciousness, which is all-pervasive (and which we all are a part of). This "sea of consciousness" is the pan-psychic field that underlies and connects all things in quantum.

Quantum reality is ambiguity bordering on intense curiosity. The physical world can seem to be a fixed, solid thing unless we transform our perceptions and regard the world with an insight into the subjectivity/objectivity of things. For instance, a common example to illustrate the quantum nature of things is that of observation/negation—regarding an object/scene physically/visually, then turning away, only to wonder whether the object/scene is still present (as it is). Of course, when you turn back to look, the object remains; however, one can never know, in the absence of observation, whether an object truly exists or not. This is the mystery of quantum physics, and this is the future of science. We, as a society, are beginning to explore uncharted territory in which the unknown will feature prominently; after all, there will always be more mystery.

I would like to state here that I am not a quantum physicist. I am a Witch who understands, embraces, and works with magick, and sees the obvious parallels between our philosophies and cosmologies and that of quantum physics. I hope that in your exploration of the cosmos (both inner and outer), your yearning and seeking will continue to avail you in the most curious of ways.

For more information on quantum physics, please see the bibliography of this book.

ENERGETIC EXERCISES
FOR THE AVID WITCH

The magickal arsenal of the Witch is a very personalised thing. It's almost like an astral toolbox that you can conjure at any moment and apply to life! I'm not talking here about physical tools that you may work with in your magickal endeavours; I'm speaking about the energetic exercises, techniques, and methods you integrate into your practice in order to increase the vital flow of energy within your being, to purify and cleanse your being, and also, simply, for play.

The Rod of Power

The rod of power is akin to the concept and metaphysics of the tree of life alignment meditation (grounding and centring). However, the dynamics of this exercise in increasing vital flow tend towards the slightly more dramatic—a lightning flash of enlightenment that restores vitality in the system.

Stand erect in a power stance (feet spread apart, aligning with hips; palms facing forward, and arms hanging casually by your sides; shoulders back and relaxed), and ground and centre using the tree of life alignment meditation.

Be open, receptive, and ready. Intone the following quickly, sharply, and with authority:

Rod of power, lightning strike! Restore my vitality!

Mentally hear a crack of thunder and see and feel the lightning bolt hit you. Feel the rush of energy as it floods your being. In your mind's eye, picture your whole self glowing. You have become the rod of power—so mote it be!

The Aura Flush

The name for this exercise began as a joke, but then the more I taught the method to people, the more the joke stuck—and thus to this day I still call it the aura flush.

Centre yourself. Visualise and feel your aura around your physical being. See it glowing in whichever colour you like. Then, once this is established, consciously expand your aura until it fills the room you are in. If you are outside, go as far as you possibly can or until you feel the need to stop. Now gather up all of the light and concentrate it just above your head in the form of an orb. This is where the "flush" part comes in. Visualise/feel the light travelling swiftly and cleanly down the front of your body, underneath your feet, up the back of your body, and then over your head. Keep the light circulating like this for as long as you like. Then, when it strikes you, take a spark of the flush and create one that circulates around the sides of your body (laterally, so to speak). As the light flows, focus on the intention to purify and cleanse your being.

As you are concentrating on your aura circulating around your physical being, you are also activating and cleansing the other energetic/psychic layers of your being, not to mention clearing out the emotional and mental aspects as well.

When you feel the work has been done, simply let your aura become as it is naturally, and ground your awareness in the physical reality once more.

Psyballs

One of my favourite things to do when I first started experimenting with energy work was to create psyballs. A psyball is a concentrated orb/sphere/ball of psychic power that is shaped through visualisation and kinesthetic sensation and imbued with particular emotions or thoughtforms. They are useful as spell-containers, which are then absorbed back into the aura for later use or placed elsewhere (somewhere memorable and psychically safe). They can also be harnessed to cast quick and effective spells when in a hurry. The following method is the one that works for me, and it is also the one I teach others; however, as with anything, feel free to adapt and personalise it to your own tastes.

Ground and centre. Gather up and call in as much energy you feel intuitively you will need to create a psyball. Visualise and feel the psyball (colour, texture, weight, etc.) you want to create as you do this. Now hold your hands (at whichever height you wish) as if you were holding a ball or sphere. Place the visualisation of the psyball between your hands, and begin to channel and direct the flow of energy into your hands. You are now energetically and psychically creating the psyball. As you direct the flow of energy, also take time to visualise your desired outcome if using the psyball for spellcraft (for immediate or later use), and inject the psyball with the necessary emotion/sensation/thoughtform for the work. However, if you are just experimenting and playing with energy, then keep the energy pure. Either way, make sure that you fill the psyball with as much energy as you can until it feels like it might burst! Then twist your hands around a few times and seal the psyball so that it doesn't leak or disperse. Affirm that the psyball is real and ready. You can now throw or pass the psyball to someone else (if you are working in a group situation) or play with it on your own. Prod and poke it and do whatever you like; this is your psyball to experiment with! If the psyball is for spellcraft, then either absorb it into your auric skin for later use or release it into the ether to do its work. You can do this by throwing the psyball into the air in whichever direction you choose and releasing the power.

MAGICK:
THE WITCH'S SACRED PRINCIPLE

Magick—the art of sensing and shaping the subtle,
unseen forces that flow through the world, of awakening
deeper levels of consciousness beyond the rational.
—Starhawk, *The Spiral Dance*

Mention Witchcraft or Witches and the mind will instantly jump to magick. Magick and Witches are irrevocably interconnected. A Witch acknowledges the life flow of our universe as innately magickal, and this "juice" not only powers our Craft, it also affirms life in its myriad expressions. I often think of magick as the Witch's most sacred principle. It is the guiding force and reality in our spirituality. Magick, like energy (as discussed above), is hard to define, but it is within all things and therefore, if one is open or willing to become open, magick is there to know and feel.

I believe that a Witch becomes a Witch when they have fully embraced and integrated an awareness of magick into their life. With awareness of magick comes the ability to work with it to accomplish goals, fulfil desires, and dance with ecstasy. With this ability and talent comes the charge of duty and responsibility. This is when ethics—personal, communal, or otherwise—become significant in a Witch's life. Ethics form the basis of how one approaches life and also how one experiences it.

Magick is not a supernatural force that allows us amoral freedom to manifest our every whim. It is important to remember that, because it is the Witch's sacred principle, magick is to be honoured and cherished as a friend and lover. Magick is not a tool; it is something that is very much alive, and we are empowered through our relationship with it.

In my book *Spirited* I discuss what I feel magick is, and I mention that it is a child of nature. If magick is the Witch's sacred principle, then nature would have to be our sacred foundation. From this blessed foundation arises magick, and because we as Witches consciously attune to the cycles and tides of nature, we are explicitly tied in with the force of magick. There is a Voudoun belief that all humans are born of magick. We are nature, and thus magick is our lifeblood! In the following section, I will outline a process whereby you can come to acknowledge magick as your most sacred principle and partner in the Craft.

Acknowledging Magick as Partner in the Craft

One does not "do" magick; one can only work, love, sing, dance, paint, eat, etc., *with* magick. It is something to be breathed and lived entirely. It encompasses and saturates all things. This is why, in those awe-inspired moments, people exclaim "Magick!" There's no other word for it. For a Witch to acknowledge magick as partner in the Craft, it is necessary to understand the vastness of this force and also its seed-fire that erupts within the ignited consciousness that is you. This is the endless journey of the wild Witch.[20]

I am a writer, and I happen to be a Witch (and vice versa), so I find myself writing about my Craft and spirituality. In book formats it is sometimes difficult to avoid the "step" syndrome, though I seem to be able to divert around it most of the time. For now, I will simply submit and allow a series of steps to unfold on the page. Following these steps wholeheartedly and with passion should lead to a truly beautiful relationship with magick.

Step 1: Acknowledge Magick as Sacred Principle

Do it. It is quite simply done. Make sure, however, that you do not base this perception solely on what you have read in books.

---

20 Witches tend to honour wildness; in the WildWood Tradition, we celebrate and embrace this fact.

Step 2: Live and Experience Magick as Sacred Principle

Live it. When you wake up in the morning, you may feel a little like I do—always okay, but sometimes a little irate at the curse of early morning shifts at work. From the moment you shower, brush your teeth, pull on your clothes for the day, and step out the door, things change. You have prepared yourself for the day ahead (whether that is work or leisure). Be eager and embrace life!

Lately I've caught some brilliant sunrises. The eastern horizon is streaked with the rosy-fingered expressions of dawn, and the morning birds are singing with zest. I am always honoured and humbled to be a part of that experience, considering most of the people whose streets I walk through are sleeping through it.

Always see the blessings; receive and live them. This is all magick! Light a candle, have a break for a moment, and breathe it all in. Let the power of it soak through every pore and saturate your being. This is the true meaning of relaxation: letting yourself be in the moment with everything else going on; it always will be. Recently, while meditating at the bus stop, I realised that I am peace moving through chaos (and chaos flows through me), and that chaos and peace live together, on top of each other all the time, and that's the way it's meant to be.

Step 3: Cultivate Magick as Sacred Principle

When you live through the cycle of flourishing, waning, dying, resting, returning, burgeoning—new life over and over—you become distinctly aware that you can cultivate life rather consciously in your own sphere of the cosmos. When you help to create fertile ground for seeds to be nourished and sustained and to eventually grow into splendour, you become an active participant within the cycles of nature—the sacred foundation. From that foundation is born magick, and thus you cultivate magick as sacred principle simply by participating in life over and over and never ceasing to change.

Step 4: Affirm Magick as Sacred Principle

Repeat steps 1–3 endlessly.

Magick is as magick is. Like the Wyrd, it is very difficult to define in any rational/logos sense, and because of this it is best left to be. We should all take a leaf from the magick book and acknowledge, live, experience, and cultivate with each breath we take. Remember to always release each cycle naturally, and then inspire a new one all over again. This is life, and life is pure magick.

8

TO FLY IN SPIRIT

Flying is learning how to throw yourself at the ground and miss.
—Douglas Adams

One of the most commonly perpetuated iconic myths regarding Witches is that we can physically fly. I will not doubt the possibility of physical flight in this book (or in my mind); however, I have never personally experienced it.[21] My experience of magickal flight lies in what is now called astral travel.

The term astral travel refers to the transportation of consciousness through the agency of the astral plane/energy to a desired location, time period, or realm. Astral travel, or astral projection, is a conscious experience of spiritual journeying that enables the individual to explore possibilities unimagined in mundane awareness. It can also happen involuntarily when one is exhausted, ill, frightened, or unfocussed in any way. There are portals through which the astral body can simply slip out. I recall a few instances while I was

---

21 I have, however, been a participant in a levitation circle and have been physically transported several metres while raising power in circle.

in high school in which I would physically fall back onto my bed or the lounge, and then instead of feeling the sensation of the physical mattress or cushion I would be hovering a metre or two above my physical self.

Astral travel was a magickal talent that I had to work hard at to become proficient in. Nowadays I am very confident in my spirit flight, as astral travel is also known, and I have found myself teaching the skill to others at various times, especially within my coven. What follows in this section is an outline of several processes through which you may achieve astral travel successfully, and also some much-needed, personalised advice on the matter.

Successful astral travel consists of these steps:

1.   Discovering your astral key
2.   Opening, balancing, and cleansing your chakras
3.   Loosening the astral body
4.   Creating an astral projection (the chariot)
5.   Transporting the astral self to the astral projection
6.   Being in and becoming the chariot
7.   Flying!

DISCOVERING YOUR ASTRAL KEY

The plethora of how-to guides on astral travel all seem to utilise similar methods of journeying. However, looking back, I realise now that there was something missing that would have helped me with my spirit flight much earlier on. Perhaps the journey of discovering my own personal key to success was worth that time and patience.

Many of us have had flying dreams; in fact, they are quite common when we are younger and developing identity and "place." The usual interpretation of a flying dream is that the dreamer is experiencing a great sense of freedom, either in their waking life or through the medium of dreaming. On reflection, I realised that in most of

my flying dreams, I was pulled into the air by a kite. In most cases, I would be standing in my front yard on a windy day, and a kite string would either materialise in front of me or fall from the sky. I'd grab hold tightly, and the next gust of wind would send me up high into the atmosphere. They were exhilarating dreams! I recalled these dreams in the period in which astral travel was high on my "learn to do" list in my senior years of high school.

The next time I attempted an astral journey, I wove the kite imagery and the sensation of the pull upwards into the methods I was using. In a manner of days, I began to experience short journeys in which I would float around my room and house. Concurrently to this, I had been doing a lot of trance journey work[22] with my goddess Persephone. Often I would travel to Mount Olympos or the underworld. My goddess had gifted me with a personal tool/symbol for empowerment and to help bring healing, wholeness, and purity to others in my life—a sword of light.

I was having a devotional circle in my garden temple at my mother's old house in Toowoomba, and I had reached the point of near-exit from the physical body when I intuitively began to visualise my sword hanging (floating horizontally outwards) in front of me. I raised as much power as I could, and in a cataclysmic burst, my astral self leapt forth and raced down the blade of the sword, and I was propelled energetically from the garden into my mother's room. It was the most successful and potent astral experience I had ever had up until that point. In the same token, a few months later, when I had just recently moved to Brisbane, my goddess Aphrodite revealed a sigil to me that I

---

22 The difference between astral travel and trance journeying is the emphasis on conscious awareness and the metaphysical transportation of the awareness that is required for the former. Trance journeying, though it also requires a loosening of the astral self, is similar to gnosis in that the consciousness expands and encompasses different realities and therefore other realms. Astral travel is designed to condense awareness into a singular vessel so that greater movement can be applied to an individuated perception. It truly does enable you to fly!

deduced instinctively was a power symbol to aid in my spirit flight. It works wonders!

I encourage anyone seeking success in spirit flight to take some time to reflect on flight dreams and also to talk with any deities/allies/totems/guides who may have wisdom to dispense. Shamanic deities like Persephone, Dionysos, Hermes, Freya, Odin, Rhiannon, and the like will offer inspiration in this area. Another idea is to incorporate any personal symbols or magickal tools/items into your visualisation of an astral key. For instance, during an all-day workshop I was running for a coven on the Gold Coast, one of the Witches present enquired whether an astral key could be something like a feather, as for her they were symbols of flight and she used them quite frequently in her magickal work. "Of course," was my answer. "Personalisation with any magickal talent will always create effective pathways to success. This is your personal key, and I suggest you seize it and fly!"

OPENING, BALANCING, AND CLEANSING YOUR CHAKRAS

When I first started researching the art of astral travel, I read a few books that suggested chakra work before the actual astral projection was to be embarked on. It made sense to me, metaphysically speaking, and so I began to really work with my chakras—opening, balancing, and cleansing them. Once I started to incorporate this focus on my chakras in my preparation for astral journeys, I began to experience much more success with the loosening of my astral body, which is absolutely necessary in achieving projection. Below is an excerpt from an unpublished article I wrote in 2006 entitled "Wheels of Life: Understanding & Working with the Chakras." The exercise below will help to open, balance, and cleanse your chakras.

Working with the Chakras:
An Exercise in "Bringing Forth"

The purpose of aligning and balancing the chakras is, in effect, to allow for the transmission of the cosmic energy between the above and the below (the heavens and the manifest, material realm that is our earth). We have made and consecrated the rod of power, and the spear of light is brought forth, searing division between all things and uniting them simultaneously. As the Kundalini rises, it brings with it a current that is initially receptive and then projective and transformed with creative love in between, and as the chakras work their way into the centre that is the heart, each respectively receives or directs the flow of energy accordingly. In doing so, a polarity and dynamism occurs in which the receptive and projective qualities are harmonised—the Masculine and the Feminine united—and arouse gnosis, which glows brightly aflame at the crown, bringing divine insight, vision, power, and peace. The chakras can also be equated to the planetary spheres of the Hermetic journey-work, which aims at stripping away each layer that coats our being to reach the inner core that is the sanctum of our own divinity.

The chakras form a ladder of ascension into higher states of consciousness through which we achieve union with the Divine, though they are all inherently equal and significant pieces of the puzzle. This is the world tree, the axis mundi, the *poto mitan* of the Voudoun tradition. It is phallic but activated and brought into being by the dynamic, wise serpent herself. If we balance, align, and channel through our chakras, we are purposefully creating a life of happiness, health, and wisdom.

- Ground and centre through rhythmic breathing while standing upright or lying down on your back.

- Focus on your being and visualise yourself as the world tree, a megalithic standing stone, or another meaningful and vivid power image that relates to the purpose at hand.

- Centre your attention at the base of your spine. Visualise a sphere of red light pulsing and spinning, unfolding to become a beautiful flower. Feel and see the link that is now forged between your base chakra and the earth. Visualise this as a glowing red cord of energy spiralling up to meet you.

- Now allow the energy to continue upward, as the sacral chakra, in its vivid orange, spins and unfolds to become a flower.

- Continue on with the appropriate colours and chakras[23] until you reach the heart chakra, where you will imbue this current of energy with unconditional, eternal love. Now direct the current with added willpower, but still allow for the natural flow.

- The light continues to grow in intensity and clarity as it passes through and is charged by each chakra (don't forget colours), finally reaching the crown and spilling forth in incandescent rays of pure white light. Allow yourself to receive the light of the heavens and let it pass through your body, joining with the earth's energy, creating a dynamic cycle of supreme polarity.

It is done.

---

23 Base chakra (base of spine)—red; sacral chakra (between pubic region and navel)—orange; solar plexus chakra (at the meeting place of the ribs)—yellow; heart chakra (in the centre of the chest)—green; throat chakra (at the throat)—sky blue; third eye chakra (in the centre of your forehead)—indigo; crown chakra (just above your head)—violet. The full article can be found at http://www.gede parma.com/?p=13.

Don't forget to ground the energy and work your way back down through the chakras, closing them off as you go and keeping them aligned. You can do this easily by reversing the order of the way in which you opened the chakras and physically tapping with your index finger each chakra three times while visualising it becoming smaller and smaller, until it is but a pinpoint of coloured light. The reverse order would be from crown to root.

In this case, however, you won't close the chakras off until you return from your astral journey, as they are helping to prepare and ignite the astral body for the flight. The sealing of the chakras occurs upon returning to the physical self.

LOOSENING THE ASTRAL BODY

Before you project the astral self, you need to loosen it. The self that you are is composed of layer upon layer of various substances and energies that coexist simultaneously and affect each other to create the synthesis, or vibration, which is the unique you. For instance, Raven Grimassi paints this picture of the seven realms of being (and thus the makeup of the body):

1. Ultimate
2. Divine
3. Spiritual
4. Mental
5. Astral
6. Elemental
7. Physical

When astral projecting, it is important to understand that it is your conscious awareness that is leaping from your physical self to the astral body you have created to be your chariot. Of course, it is theorised that the actual substance that is energetically transporting is astral. In the end, occult theories don't really matter, as long as you can do the job effectively and be better for it!

To loosen the seat of awareness from being squarely within the body to going beyond, one must raise the power that exists within the self to heighten the vibrations, which ideally creates a portal through which the leap can happen. The chakra exercise and the aura flush given above can help you in this area. Another option would be to take the chakra exercise further and weave the energy channeling of the aura flush in with it. For example, after each chakra has been opened, balanced, and cleansed, begin to spin them all faster and faster until you feel as if you yourself are spinning around and around. You will begin to feel waves of magnetic pulsations ride across you as you continue spinning the chakras. It's all just a matter of exciting the energy that lies latent within you to the point of frenzy. When the power has been raised to this point of frenzy, many people find that suddenly the energy jars and won't go any further. Great disappointment can be felt—I know, I have felt it. Don't let this get you down; simply learn from it! Many people fear the intensity of such a potent energetic experience. However, go with the flow and ride it out. The next time you begin to raise the power to loosen the astral self, trust in the experience and know that you are safe and protected. Affirm this in your mind by calling on the guardianship of your deities and spiritual allies. If you succeed in projecting, they will oversee the journey for you, and they will also add their own divine inspiration and encouragement as you engage with these methods.

It is important to understand that loosening the astral self is vital to spirit flight. Without the ability to raise power and to excite the vibration to create the necessary portal through which the leap is made, astral projection cannot happen.

CREATING AN ASTRAL PROJECTION (THE CHARIOT)

To be able to actually fly in the spirit, one needs a medium, a vessel, through which to do it. In the Aurum Solis magickal (theurgic) tradition,[24] this medium is called the chariot. I use the term also because the method for astral projection outlined in the *Mysteria Magica* books was one of the few published astral techniques that helped me to achieve success in spirit flight.

To create a chariot is as simple as visualising a light etheric double[25] in front of you or hovering just above your physical body. Construct the visual reality in your mind, and then energise and lend it vitality and substance by sending astral power to charge and actualise it. This process will forge the psychic link necessary for you to take the next step and make the great leap!

TRANSPORTING THE ASTRAL SELF TO THE ASTRAL PROJECTION

When transporting the conscious awareness of self to the astrally created chariot, one needs to gather the energy of awareness in a single place. Most people will naturally be inclined to pool the energy at the chakra point that is most sensitive to personalised magickal work. Generally, when astral projecting, my awareness will sit at my third eye, heart, or solar plexus chakras. Once the energy of conscious awareness is gathered in a power place, it becomes concentrated and the vibration will heighten, or quicken. This arouses the excitement even more so. The key at this stage is not to lose to doubt or fear. Just go with the flow and maintain a lucid awareness of the goings-on.

---

24 Melita Denning and Osborne Phillips are the carriers-on of the Hermetic Ogdoadic Tradition. The Order Aurum Solis, which was founded in 1897 and exists today, is the leading exponent of this ancient magickal philosophy.

25 Duplicate yourself; however, to create flow of movement, make sure that you are viewing your back (of the chariot/double) from your vantage point.

At the right moment, you will feel the pressure climax, and that is the time to take the risk and make the great leap. It is like a mental jump—from Point A (the power place) to Point B (the chariot). The leap should be swift, almost instantaneous. It should transport the entirety of your conscious awareness in no time to your chariot.

If you feel you have failed the first time, keep on leaping until you can affirm that you've made the transition. The first success you have may not be so apparent to you, as it is often a very surreal feeling to inhabit an astrally built vessel and wander around in it for the first time. It may even feel as if you are in two places at once. If this happens, place more focus on your astral awareness, and the spirit flight itself should be great! Remember to trust your intuition and to go with the flow.

BEING IN AND BECOMING THE CHARIOT

Once inside the chariot, you will feel the need to adjust to your new environment. Many people experience a "fluffy" response to the world around them, or a vibratory, atmospheric fluttering sensation. However, the experience is unique for everyone.

Make sure you affirm consciously that you have imbued the chariot with your vital charge (astrally) and thus have enabled it to act as a projection of yourself. You will now be able to expand and enhance your senses and channel with them to receive new information about the cosmos. With spirit flight, the same physical limitations imposed on our mortal bodies do not apply. We are able to fly to the far reaches of the universe and travel anywhere we can imagine.

Be in your chariot—*be* your chariot! At first, you may feel as if you are imagining everything and that therefore it isn't real or of substance. Truthfully, much of astral travel is powered by the imagination in the first place! You need to be able to dream and see (and know!) the story before it becomes possible. The cosmos has a beautiful way of unravelling and revealing truth when we reflect on the possibility that something is true—even more so when we act as if it is true.

When it comes to travelling, viewing, and experiencing in your chariot, do not overexert your control mentality. Do not push for things to happen; just let things happen naturally. They will and they do.

It is also essential that the rational, everyday, cautionary prohibitions of mortal living don't overcrowd your astral experience. Abstain from judgment, analysis, and evaluation; leave that for later. Simply trust in your intuition to keep you safe and protected, and instinctually know the benevolent from the malevolent when it comes to encountering other entities out there. Remember: not everything wishes the best for you! However, if you are the type to worry about these things, then make sure you understand the risks completely before attempting astral travel, and if you do go ahead with spirit flight, then call upon the aid of your guides/totems/deities/etc. to watch over you as you travel. When you are ready to return to your physical self, simply think of it, and you will find yourself sliding back into your body. When your consciousness reabsorbs into your physical self, so will the astral chariot and the excess substance you projected, as it all originally belonged to you in the first place. Affirm this for yourself just to make sure. Click into place, and allow time for readjustment and grounding.

FLYING!

Spirit flight is an amazing skill to possess. Like any skill, it only improves with practice. It's not about perfection; it's not an exact science. However, if you follow the method outlined above (or any other technique you feel drawn to use) and do so with passion, a desire for success, and integrity, then there is no doubt that you will soar!

There are many metaphysical theories that detail the delicate nature of the astral realm and what it is to project and travel with and through it. I have never really given it much thought beyond its existence, the implications thereof, and how these may affect my spirit flight. I don't really try to paint otherworldly geographies whereby these different realms are given structure through division and labelling. My advice is not to worry so much where you go but *how* you go.

There are so many wondrous and ecstatic experiences to be had in spirit—so many realms, worlds, and possibilities to explore! You can even stay on this plane and visit the country or sacred site of your choice. I remember exploring the ruins of the temple grounds at Eleusis before I physically visited in October 2008. The astral experience matched vividly with my physical presence at the temple grounds. However, when I flew in spirit to Eleusis, the buildings themselves were not in ruins, as they are today. I have also flown through what seemed to be Salem, Massachusetts (USA), and I've had many an adventure around the land of Oz. The possibilities are infinite, and to use that old cliché, the only limit is your imagination!

9

TO SEE CLEARLY

I also learned to see, and this was a different
kind of seeing which came first by night.
—Vivianne Crowley, *Phoenix from the Flame*

Clairvoyance means "clear sight," and therein lies the inspiration for
this chapter's title. I am fortunate enough to have been born into a
family in which these psychic gifts of clear sight (or "the Sight") have
always been nurtured and promoted. I remember instances when I
lived at home with my mother when people would ask for readings
and guidance, and, as I was only a young teenager (and sometimes a
lazy one), I would try to weasel out of it. Both my father and mother
would urge me to read, as they knew that we would all get something
out of it and it would only increase my psychic skill. This hereditary
lineage of the Sight (our gift) hit home when, during my 2008 trip to
Bali, I was reading for about five women at my aunt's place and one of
my relatives mentioned to my mother that it was obvious I had inher-
ited my abilities from my late Balinese grandmother.

I have written and spoken about my grandmother many times
before, and it is often a strange revelation when people discover that

she passed when I was two. I only have vague, almost ethereal memories of her physical self, but she is ever-present in my life, and because of the blessed gifts she passed through my father to me, I have always been in contact with her. In high school, when my life was in emotional turmoil, she appeared to me as a frenzied, fiery serpent woman. There are many reasons for this, but generally I believe she manifested in this way to effectively grab my attention! (It worked.)

I had already developed the ability to see auras in their fullness when I was fourteen, and soon after, my grandmother decided to fire up my life as my clairvoyant talent accelerated, and I began seeing and communicating with spirits on a weekly basis. I became so utterly intuitive that every reading I did (palms, cards, scrying, etc.) proved dramatically accurate for the querent. This increased my confidence in my abilities, and thereby I transcended any barrier of doubt. I learnt that the art of divination and of being an oracle is essentially about cultivating oneself as a vessel. As a vessel, one receives the constant flow of fate and learns the art of interpretation. All of this must be tempered with intuition and instinct, however, or the personalised meaning and significance of the wisdom lose their relevance.

In this chapter, I will use the term *clairvoyance* rather openly. There are many psychics (and this is not a word I often use to describe myself) who describe themselves as clairsentient (clear sensing), clairaudient (clear hearing), claircognizant (clear knowing), clairalient (clear smelling), and the list goes on. Throughout this chapter/book, when I use the word *clairvoyance* I will generally be referring to all of the above and more. Clairvoyance, at least to me, tends to cover the full range of "knowing"[26] psychic gifts. However, for the sake of specificity, I will tend to focus on the Sight, as this is my area of expertise.

---

26 I see, therefore I know; I hear, therefore I know; I smell, therefore I know; I sense, therefore I know; I taste, therefore I know.

TO OPEN THE THIRD EYE

The third eye has become somewhat of a New Age cliché in the twenty-first century. Its popularity supersedes the other chakras by far! Unfortunately, the overstated adoration of this energy centre has tainted the reality of this highly important chakra. The relevance of the third eye to clairvoyance is an obvious one. The name of the chakra itself gives a symbolic hint as to the function of this energy centre. The third eye, or the mind's eye, is that "other" sight mechanism that enables the individual to receive wisdom and information that would otherwise escape the physical eyes/sight. Developing and enhancing the potency of the third eye expands psychic awareness and allows for the free flow of information.

The important thing to remember with opening the third eye is that the more gradual the process, the better. Like any magickal work, it's best not to rush in for the sake of acquiring a new power. The journey is what counts; if gifts develop along the way, it's merely a bonus! However, learning to flex your muscles is never a bad thing and helps to keep the self healthy and balanced. Always remember to give and receive in equal measure.

Although I cannot profess to completely understand the metaphysics and the science behind clairvoyance, I do have several intuitions regarding the nature of the Sight. Firstly, those who "see" will all perceive differently. Generally, when I clairvoyantly perceive something, whether it be a spirit, deity, aura, or totem, I will see it just as I see things in the physical realm; I would articulate this as "apparent" Sight. The vision/being appears quite vividly for me. However, often I will also perceive with what many call the mind's eye. I see and know that what I am sensing is definitely there; however, I can only give it form or sensation within my mind. There are many degrees of differing versions of clairvoyance between and beyond these two ways; however, in essence, all sight is Sight. Remember that physical sight is merely the outcome of the reflection of light. The mind tends to rule perception.

To flex this particular psychic muscle (the third eye), you will need to centre and expand your consciousness in whichever way you prefer. As your awareness grows to encompass the beyond, and your inner tides surrender to the being of cosmos, embrace the current of life as a concentrated beam of light that flows directly through and into your third eye (the area on your forehead between and just above your eyebrows). You will feel a slight pressure, tingle, or buzz on the physical area. Concentrate on amplifying this sensation, and place the focus of your awareness in this area. Acknowledge and affirm that you are ready and prepared to receive fate/Wyrd/information in the form of a "knowing" (vision, scent, words, cognizance, etc.), and surrender to the flow. Allow whatever you perceive to simply be—and do not judge, evaluate, or analyse what it is you are receiving. Let it unravel in its own way before you impose any personalisation upon it. Of course, after the experience, the discernment tools of judgment, evaluation, and analysis will prove very useful; however, make sure you regard the experience with intuition first.

TO SEE IN APPARENCE[27]

When people think of "having the Sight" or "possessing the Gift," it is generally surmised that the seer will perceive the Other in apparence—in a vivid, raw, "right in front of the face" way. Upon closer inspection, clairvoyance does not always necessarily work like this. In fact, many clairvoyants/seers/psychics will perceive with the mind's eye, as mentioned above. In truth, there is no difference in validity between seeing in "apparence" and seeing in the mind.

---

27 The word *apparence* is not considered by the dictionaries to be an English word; however, for ease of flow within the text, I choose this form of spelling rather than the technically correct *apparentness*. *Apparence* is a French word that translates into English as "appearance."

There are a variety of metaphysical and occult explanations regarding how one technically perceives with the Sight. As has been made obvious throughout this book, I am not one to dabble in or be devoted to what the Pagan author John J. Coughlin terms "pseudo-metaphysics," which he defines as "the assumption of truth based on what sounds as if it could be true."[28] In saying this, however, vibrational frequency has been touted as a way to explain the contrast between apparence and mind sight within the realms of clairvoyance. This theory tends to hold some sway in magickal circles, as the concept of energy vibration is quite a well-articulated and accepted one. In fact, the concept has even been measured and recorded scientifically (as in the works of Richard Gerber), and vibrational frequencies have been proven to underlie our conscious and subconscious perceptions of things.

Discarnate, discrete entities and beings have no physical bodies and therefore are composed of pure, unhindered, concentrated energy, flowing without stricture or strain. Therefore, most human beings are not able to physically perceive these entities, as our vibration is grounded in the physical and we have been indoctrinated to wholly believe that the physical is the only realm of existence. Only through concentrated and continued work can we alter our consciousness to allow for the reception of higher vibrational frequencies (faeries, devas, angels, deities, etc.). Of course, in magickal work it is necessary to raise power, and this is synonymous with increasing vibrational frequency. This is why, when we are directly engaging with these powerful forces, we are more prone to seeing Other phenomena and, as the Christians would say, witnessing miracles.

Magickally adept people—those who flow with the tides and rhythms of the pure will of nature/cosmos/life and embrace the All that dwells within—are completely capable of raising power and thus cultivating the Sight. All of the exercises provided within this book,

---

28 John J. Coughlin, *Ethics and the Craft* (USA: Waning Moon Publications, 2009).

from breathwork to astral travel, will enable you to achieve the state of consciousness needed for developing these skills.

Therefore, if you wish to have the awe-inspiring experience of perceiving in apparence, then all you must do is increase your vibration, relax, and receive. By raising power for a spell—or singing, chanting, dancing, making love, etc.—you are creating the right conditions for developing this extra dimension of your clairvoyance.

TO BECOME STILL

Om mani padme hum
—Tibetan Buddhist mantra

Another important perspective when regarding clairvoyance—or life in general—is the teaching of stillness.

Stillness is considered to be a sacred technique of attaining enlightenment in many Eastern traditions. In many European Pagan traditions, it seems as if stillness is rejected for active techniques of altering consciousness (e.g., visualisation); however, stillness permeates our philosophies.

In many creation myths, at the core of all things and "in the beginning" is chaos—that dark chasm of undifferentiated potential. It is life, before life ever conceived of itself. Chaos then gave birth to cosmos, and from cosmos comes all that we can behold. This concept was consolidated for me while I was sitting at the bus stop. I was breathing and centring myself, and the image of a lotus floating peacefully on a lake arose in my mind. I understood then the principal lesson of the Tibetan "Om mani padme hum" mantra—"I am the jewel in the lotus," and the lotus is the jewel (the peace) in the lake (the chaos)—it is all one! Peace resides perfectly within chaos, because there is no extremity in the matter; it is not a duality! Truly understanding this concept so that it began to resonate in my being opened up an awareness of underlying stillness, which permeated my entire consciousness. It was a beautiful experience and its message gives context to how I feel most of the time.

Cultivating stillness is quite a simple thing to do once you have learnt the art of sacred breath and grounding and centring. These practical techniques not only introduce the individual to the concept and reality of energy, but they also help to create space within the consciousness to arouse and connect with the stillness of being. I call this space "the void." For me, it's that consciousness of unconsciousness that stimulates the awareness into a oneness with the All-Self that is the mystery. This "oneness" (unity) can only be described as the 0 (zero) state. It is no-thing, all things, eternity looping forever without end and without beginning. Stillness is an inspiring thing!

Never try for stillness—just be it. It is not about emulating a Buddhist monk in Zen or becoming a hermit in the wilderness. Stillness is here and now, and it can be realised and made true for you.

To be still is to be completely open to the powers that be and therefore their decidedly conscious connection with our own sphere of being, and also with the channels that allow communication to and from. The most direct channel for this kind of communication would be the Sight and the clairvoyant faculties. Cultivating stillness enhances the efficacy and the clarity of the visions and intuitions received through Sight.

VISION INTERPRETATION: LITERAL VERSUS SYMBOLIC

A common pitfall that can hamper even the most experienced seer is whether a vision can be trusted as a literal representation of a reality which will emerge (or has emerged or is emerging) or whether it is symbolic. For example, I once had a vision in the staff bathroom at my old workplace; I looked into the mirror while washing my hands, and my face morphed into a crocodile's head. Upon returning to work, a customer approached the counter and before anything else was said or done, he placed a rather large novelty crocodile head in front of me. I laughed at the irony and strangeness of the whole experience! An example of a symbolic interpretative vision would be seeing a rooster (a symbol of sexuality and resurrection) impressed on someone's auric field. One could then go on to tell this person that they need to focus on re-empowering and revitalising their sexual drive.

There is a fine line between literal and symbolic interpretations, as you could just as easily see my crocodile vision as being further punctuated by the appearance of a physical crocodile head in my material reality, and therefore a deeper insight into the symbolic nature of the crocodile may be revealed. Similarly, to see a rooster in someone's aura might not be merely symbolic—it could also mean that Rooster (the animal totem) may be wholly dwelling with this individual for a time. Another personal example that highlights this fine line rather perfectly is a vision I had of the Egyptian god Anubis floating down a river in a boat. I then read an article a week later that documented the floating of a statue of Anubis down the Thames River in London to celebrate the opening of a new Egyptian exhibit. Despite the official journalistic record, many mystics and occultists commented that this event signalled the opening up of a new age and the return of the Old Gods.

My advice is to not worry too much concerning what kind of vision it is or how to interpret it. Simply be open to possibility and trust in the intuitive guidance of Spirit; all will unravel as it should.

EXERCISING AND DEVELOPING THE SIGHT

There are many methods, techniques, and exercises you can work with in order to develop your propensity for clairvoyance. As with anything, it is practice that makes perfect—or in this case, psychic.

Here are two Sight-strengthening and -developing exercises, as well as a clairvoyant-clarifying eyewash and advice on scrying.

Beyond all else, the key to obtaining the Sight lies within the power of observation. Everything in existence is here to behold; simply become observant of the subtler things in life, and you will become receptive to the Other.

Seeing Auras

The aura is considered by many Witches to be the life energy of each thing projected externally—the inner flame radiating outwards into the world. The aura has been subject to much theorising concerning its various layers and how they each connect with a specific realm of existence or chakra/energy centre. The only way this can affect seeing auras depends on how acute one's Sight is, and therefore whether one is able to see the entire aura or only the etheric body (closest to the skin). The etheric body is surrounded by the mental/emotional aura, which is then surrounded by the spiritual aura. Janet Farrar and Gavin Bone teach that there are seven layers of the aura, which correspond to the seven major chakras; however, it is generally accepted that most seers and psychics will only be able to see the three mentioned above.

There are various psychic exercises already in circulation that, if practised regularly and with conviction, will enable the individual to see the aura. Here, I will merely add my personal experience and advice to the plethora of information out there already.

I first began to see auras when I was in year 9 of high school. I remember gazing in a relaxed state at my health and physical education teacher, who would pace back and forth in front of the whiteboard while talking to the class. Eventually his body would become encased in an azure blue egg of light. At first I didn't really pay attention or think anything of it—until I realised it was his aura. After this experience, I began to see auras around most of my teachers, but also around anyone whom I would look at for a short period of time. I came to understand that the best conditions for seeing auras intentionally were gazing at the object/person/creature against a neutral background and doing so in a relaxed, unaffected way, remembering that it was okay to blink!

I tend to go through periods in which I see auras regularly, without having to try; however, if someone asks me to look at their aura, or if I wish to check up on someone's health (in all aspects), I will merely enter a relaxed state and ask the person to stand against a white wall, against a tree, or lie on the ground. People tend to oblige—after all, auras tend to be of interest to most people. If this is not possible, I simply tune in and open my awareness to receive.

People often ask whether different lighting affects my Sight of auras and whether or not I can see auras at night and in the dark. I can see auras at night (though it can be more difficult), and lighting sometimes does affect my ability to see auras; however, it tends to be mostly bright, iridescent light that obscures my Sight, and the more natural the lighting, the better I see. I can only guess that this is different for everyone, although in most cases I have noticed the general similarity between different people's experiences.

Seeing the Fey

The Fey, faeries, the Good Neighbours, the Shining Ones, devas, nature spirits…different theories relegate each title to a discrete otherworldly race; others say these are all different names for the same beings. As with so many things in the magickal world/s, one needs to intuit their way through the tangled wilderness at times, then reflect, ponder, dance/sing/laugh/make love—and learn! I use the term Fey just as I would use the term Pagan—as an umbrella term that simultaneously encompasses several different groupings.

The word *Fey* derives from the English *fee*, which is connected and synonymous in meaning to the Greek *fatua* and the Latin *fata*. All of this connects the Fey (the faeries, the Good Folk) with those natural spirits who are completely in tune with and intimately conscious of the woven Wyrd that is. For this reason, time is irrelevant when it comes to the Fey, or at least stretched, warped, or Other. For instance, one evening in Faerie can measure 100 years in the mortal realm, or so they say. While I have seen the Fey quite a few times, I sense them quite regularly, especially in those raw moments and in raw places. I have had good, enlightening experiences with the Fey, and I have also had disturbing ones. In fact, I have had the pleasure— though I hardly remember the incident (as generally is the case)—of being inhabited by a faerie one Beltaine a few years ago; apparently I did a lot of giggling, ludicrous joking, and nose-picking. I have had the pleasure of seeing the legendary Tuatha De Danaan (Shining Ones), the Y Tylwyth Teg (the Welsh faerie race), Brownies (the short, brown, hairy helpers) and a gnome (red-capped), amongst other races, and all in their native habitats: Ireland, Wales, Scotland, and Brisbane (Queensland, Australia)! For the course of this section and for ease of flow, I have decided to include all of the above and more as "Fey" and "Faerie."

There are various herbs that can aid in opening one's Sight to the Fey, such as eyebright, hawthorn, and willow—and by all means, work with these helpers to assist you in your endeavours. As with any plant ally, it is important to do some initial research on the active pharmacological constituents within each herb if you wish to ingest it. In magickal work, we first and foremost work with the vibrational energy and imprint of the allies we invite in; therefore, you may simply carry a physical part (branch, leaf, berry, root, flowers, etc.) of the plant with you (on your person) to receive the magickal properties for the intended purpose.

I feel the best way to approach the Fey initially is to do just that. Open yourself to their force and their presence, acknowledge and revel in it, and declare aloud that you wish to work more closely with them. You can set this intention for a period (e.g., one lunar cycle), or you can be free with your experience and endear them that way, because the Fey are fond of no-time and aren't all that willing to acquiesce to a human's organisational inclinations; the very idea would be an anathema to them.

I often describe my own personal path as a blending of Celtic, Balinese, Greek, and Faerie traditions. This all colours my foundation as a Witch who is influenced by various traditions of Witchcraft, some modern, some older. In my weekly devotional circle, it has become my tradition (and has been for five years) to bless sweets to the Fey, as much lore attests to their love of sugar, honey, and milk. I offer sesame snaps coated in luxurious dark chocolate—a gift that totally agrees with my ethics as a vegan, and I know the Fey absolutely adore them. A true sacrifice or offering must be something that you too love. It would be no use to offer the Fey a cinnamon donut if you personally abhor donuts, as the Fey would tend to think upon this gift as one given without thought or kindness.

Just as in the Craft, it must be remembered that the gifts derived from magickal work with the Fey (e.g., being able to see them) are not necessarily the goal, they are bonuses, and we should not make them the focus of our spiritual lives. Simply be close with the wild energies of the Fey, and decorate your house and garden with bright colours (flowers, beads, and shiny things). Consider creating an altar or shrine specifically for the Fey to find rest and nourishment at. The rest will naturally come.

And just for fun, here is a chant to call the Fey to make themselves known:

> *Glittering wings and orbs of light,*
> *Let me see faeries, bring me the Sight.*

Clairvoyant-Clarifying Eyewash

The herbs used in this eyewash owe their inclusion to my good friend and fellow WildWood Witch Becky, who is currently studying for a health degree in naturopathy at Endeavour College of Natural Health in Brisbane, Queensland.

You will need the following herbs and materials:

- **Herbs:** Celery seed, dandelion root, eyebright, flax seed, and star anise (also, mugwort and wormwood to burn in an incense compound as you create the eyewash).
- **Material:** One teaspoon, two medium-sized jugs/bowls, a piece of cheesecloth, and a kettle (to boil the water with).

To make an eyewash, you will first need to create a clean eyebath. The eyebath can be a sink that you have washed with warm, soapy water and then rinsed with boiling water, or it could be a good-sized portable vessel (clean this one too). Now boil water again to fill the eyebath/vessel and place all the herbs (one teaspoon each) in the water. Allow between 15 and 20 minutes for the herbs to infuse. As the herbs infuse in the water, light the mugwort and wormwood incense, and say the following chant:

> *Witch's Sight,*
> *Second Sight,*
> *Upon my brow*
> *May Sight alight!*

Wait for another 15–20 minutes for the water to be cool enough to bathe (splash) the eyes with. Scoop up some of the infusion into a medium-sized jug or bowl, and use a piece of cheesecloth to strain the liquid into another vessel, from which you will begin the bathing. Bathe the eyes for approximately 30 seconds, then pat dry gently.

Scrying: Visions through Reflection

Scrying is the art of seeing visions and receiving intuitions through the medium of a reflective surface. The physical medium could be a dark mirror, a flame, or a bowl of dark water. Once again, as with any form of divination or clairvoyance, the way one receives, or sees, differs between each person. I generally see visual images and symbols either form in the receptacle (the mirror, the flame, or the water) or in my mind's eye, which has been stimulated by the reflective surface. Others will suddenly have peculiar thoughts for no apparent reason or a subtle sense of knowing will be aroused. It really doesn't matter how it works, only that it does.

For the following exercise, obtain a scrying receptacle and enter a meditative state. Gaze into the receptacle and breathe deeply and slowly, gradually deepening your state as you look into and through the surface of the receptacle and not directly at it. For example, if you are working with a dark mirror, gaze into its depths and not at the glass. Look at the mirror as a window into another world, and eventually you will feel as if you are falling into it. Likewise with candle scrying: gaze into the flame, and in your mind's eye see it grow tall and wavering as it consumes you. Become the flame. This principle can be applied to any medium. Simply dissolve into its presence and force, and become one with the flow of fate. Through this altered state of consciousness, we are able to know and to see. As my good friend Ana James would say, "If you know, you know; if you see, you see."

10

RITUAL

This ritual can be celebrated either as a solitary or with a group. It is a Neopagan ritual with Celtic, Wiccan, and Witchcraft influences.

You will need:

- One white taper candle
- Incense made up of 3 drops jasmine essential oil, 1 part crushed oak leaf, and 2 parts myrrh
- Brazier and charcoal disc
- Personal wishes written on cards of paper
- Ribbon

The sky ritual will work best if it is carried out beneath a tree. You can choose to set up an altar, but in this case, simplicity is key.

Ground and Centre

Ground and centre using the tree of life alignment meditation. Now, in this calm and centred state, verbally acknowledge the indigenous guardians and spirits of the place, and ask for their blessings on the ritual. Now it is time to form the space (to cast the circle).

Cast the Circle

The circle will be cast by all present holding out their power arm/ hand to the envisioned boundary of the circle and directing and channeling power to demarcate the space. This is done until the circle can be keenly felt.

At the right time, the circle should be affirmed:

> *The circle is cast. I/We are now*
> *between the worlds, in all the worlds.*
> *So mote it be.*

Acknowledge Land, Sky & Sea

If alone, make all three gestures independently while mentally or verbally acknowledging the corresponding realm. In a group situation, appoint three different people to a respective realm (one for land, one for sky, and one for sea). The gestures and words for each realm are as follows:

Land: Place both hands on the ground—*"By the land…"*

Sky: Hold hands open and up to the sky—*"By the sky…"*

Sea: Cup both hands together in front of the navel—*"And by the sea…"*

All together, say, *"By the ancient trinity, so mote it be!"*

To seal the blessing, trace a triquetra ( ) in the air with the first two fingers of your power/dominant hand.

The candle (which is placed at the foot of the tree) is lit to represent the fire of the Divine, where the three realms are one.

Blessing of the Sky

Now is the time to tie your wishes with ribbon to the tree. As you do this, understand that you are placing your trust in the greater Divine to manifest this for you in your life in whichever way is deemed most beneficial for you. As you secure the ribbon tightly, affirm in your mind the power you have to change your reality/consciousness at will.

If you are celebrating this ritual with a group, you may stand (or appoint someone else) as challenger, and recite the following charge as inspiration before the wishes are tied to the tree:

My sisters and brothers in the sky, I bless you in the name of the limitless universe, which is all things and which we all comprise. Like the core of being that is as the gaping chasm of chaos and the all-encompassing, expansive reflection of light born from the void, we become as we are. I pray that, in return, you will always seek to inspire the minds of the many and encourage the pursuit of truth as a noble work. If this is your most sacred will, this is the time to make it known. Tie your wish to the world tree and affirm it as reality.

Guided Sky Meditation

The effervescent, luminous shine of the limitless heavens arches over you as you lie upon soft grass in a vast field. All is silent; within, you feel the hum of the celestial spheres—their music, harmony, and vibration sing in your veins. Watch as the starry veil, the deep vault of the cosmos, becomes an all-encompassing, velvet-indigo flag that flutters across the sky. You feel your mind's yearning to expand and open to directly receive the divine inspiration of the Great Above.

A soft breeze gently stirs the periphery of your mind, and you feel yourself take flight. Wings lift your memory and thought high into the atmosphere, and you feel as light as a feather as the wind of the Shining Ones speeds your way.

Light…soft, delicate ripples of flowing mystery glide through the campfires of the dark cosmos. Despite the seemingly cavernous void of the heavens, there is also much to be felt and experienced. But, for now, you rest in the gentle cradle of the dark womb of Life. It is the blessed Celestial Mother who nurtures and holds you now. The weaver of the light of stars fashions a quilt to lie over your smooth, luminescent skin. She whispers to you of the wisdom of ages, which is as sand through an hourglass to her boundless being. She shares your laughter, and you smile the deep, knowing smile of the great mystery.

A feather, an eagle, a wise old sage…a star, a sun, a moon, a tendril of galaxies spiralling in on itself…wonder, awe, hope, and delight…all are held within the embrace of the sky. You pluck each thing from the vault of heaven like fruit from the world tree and carry them away with you in the carriage of memory. It is not time to drink from the well in the Deep Below; for now, just be in this moment of serenity. Release, freedom, peace, and bliss—these are the gifts of the woven magick of eternity. Here, in the realm of sky, "forever" can be witnessed.

Raise and Release the Power

To raise the power in this ritual, you will be loosening the astral body and spinning deosil, increasing the speed and vibration as you go until you are spinning above the physical ground and moving in a blur. As you are doing this, think only of your wish becoming a reality. At an intuited time, release the power, and with a definite "click," return to your physical body and ground with the earth.

Open the Space

Snuff out the candle flame and acknowledge the blessings of the three realms, the world tree that joins them, and the indigenous guardians and spirits of place. Open the circle by moving widdershins and visualising the sphere of light dispersing into the air and the earth. Do this in silence, as this can help to ground the excess energy that your body may retain after magickally intensive work. Leave the wishes tied to the tree for at least three hours, and then gather them up, burn them, and scatter the ashes to the winds. Eat and drink something to further ground the body.

SEa

part
three

CORRESPONDENCES

Classical Element	Water
Shamanic World	Underworld
Themes	Change/transformation, death/dying (the journey across the sunless sea), depth of mystery, dissolution, the quest for/of love, separation and unity as one, timelessness
Cultural/Esoteric Symbols	The cauldron of the gifts of the Tuatha De Danann, the Holy Grail, cup/chalice of the Craft tools, scallop shell (the "birth of Venus"), waves, the womb
Herbs/Plants	Aloe, avocado, belladonna, birch, cardamom, chamomile, coconut, comfrey, crocus, daffodil, dittany of Crete, elder, elm, eucalyptus, feverfew, gardenia, heather, hyacinth, iris, lilac, lily, maidenhair, moonwort, myrtle, orchid, peace, rose, rosemary, sandalwood, spearmint, thyme, valerian, vanilla, willow, yarrow, yew
Colours	Aquamarine, deep blue, purple, silver, turquoise, white

11

TO TRANCE

Watching the clouds sail above, I merged a little with the earth.
—Vivianne Crowley, *Phoenix from the Flame*

BRAIN WAVES:
FROM BETA TO DELTA

Before I get into the magickal process and philosophy of trance in the Craft traditions, I would like to bring your attention to the awesome power of brain waves. In my practice, I find it helpful to be aware of the scientific or objective foundation of a variety of important principles and philosophies integral to the heart of the Craft.[29]

There have been quite a few modern studies and research programs that have investigated the neural patterning that allows for trance in the human experience.[30] The brain conducts its activity in terms of

---

29 I pay attention only so that I am aware of mundane discourse on such things and the crossover (how, why, and when) into the realm of metaphysics. These days, however, for good or ill, the boundaries have become more and more blurred between what is classed as purely science and what we embrace as magickal.

30 Electroencephalography (EEG) is a science that records the brain's spontaneous electrical activity over short periods of time. EEG categorises neural frequencies (brain waves) according to biological symptoms experienced by the patient and spatially oriented/distinctive activity across the scalp of the patient that can be measured.

electrical frequencies/waves and thus, according to science, medicine, psychology, and metaphysics, the various levels of brain-wave activity have been categorised accordingly. The four distinctive and main brain-wave cycles are known as beta, alpha, theta, and delta, rated from highest to lowest brain-wave cycles per second. In layperson's terms, beta is mundane awareness and delta is supreme unconsciousness (e.g., a coma).

The mediating states of alpha and theta are progressively trancier, if you will. Alpha activities include mild meditation, reading, and studying. The mental processes are engaged; however, the boundaries of consciousness begin to blur. In the theta brain-wave state, we experience deeper trance states that are a helpful facilitator for spirit flight, as it becomes quite easy to dissociate and disengage from physical sensations experienced within the body. Edain McCoy equates theta state to "medium to deep sleep,"[31] and I highly recommend the section on brain waves in *Advanced Witchcraft*.

TO ENTRANCE

The most powerful work takes place when there is a combination of chanting and singing, together with the body work. This may be further enhanced by closing my eyes and receiving visionary experience. The more sensory channels that work together, the less one's self is in the way and the more intense the experience.
—Bradford Keeney, *Shaking Out the Spirits*

There are as many ways of entering trance (entrancing) as there are trancers in the world. Before embarking on such a journey, one needs to consider the variety of situations and incidents that could occur if certain preparatory procedures and safe practices are ignored.

Just as beginner Witches are taught that casting a circle is an essential ritualistic step to avoid negative psychic intrusion that may be attracted by the magickal work being carried out within the space, so

---

31 *Advanced Witchcraft: Go Deeper, Reach Further, Fly Higher* (Llewellyn, 2004), 76.

too must the willing trancer develop an awareness of the finer details of the otherworlds. However, there is no need to become overly wary concerning trance journeys/states; a simple metaphorical "look to the left, look to the right" should suffice! The cosmos isn't swarming with demonic forces looking to destroy your immortal soul, as certain Christian fundamentalists would have you believe.

A few pointers:

- Always consider your body's physical warmth and comfort prior to entering trance. When the vital life-charge journeys forth from (or expands out of) the condensed vessel that is the mortal coil, the body is left in a weaker state and becomes vulnerable to easily-dealt-with environmental conditions, e.g., temperature and hard floors. Pillows, bedding, jumpers/sweaters, and comfortable garments in general are all great trancey necessities!

- When journeying through other realms or perceiving unusual or even disturbing (from the mundane point of view) phenomena, attempt to remain receptive and casual (so as to learn and absorb proffered wisdom and insight), unless inspired to respond otherwise. I once accidentally astralled into the path of the Greek god of war, Ares. He looked intent on spiflicating whatever or whoever was behind me; I merely happened to materialise directly in front of him. I pondered flying off but quickly realised I could not simply slip away unaffected. So, remaining true to my convictions, I simply knelt beneath his enraged and gleaming red eyes and held my hands in the Balinese prayer pose my father taught me,[32] while chanting "peace,

---

32 Palms and fingers pressed together and held slightly above and in front of the crown of the head.

peace, peace" over and over. It seemed to pacify the god, and I escaped unscathed.

- In other cases, however, you will experience situations in which you are unable to simply assume the role of awkward bystander; often you will have to interact! These points of interaction can create powerful synergy and thus portals into deeper awareness of what or who the being/ symbol embodies. Gnosis is attained in many ways during psychic-trance communion with the deities, spirits, and miscellaneous entities of the otherworlds.

- Whatever your personal opinion or belief on the matter, make sure you treat the worlds you explore and the beings you encounter as real. If not, you are likely to miss out on seeing and understanding the wisdom contained within the experience, or, slightly worse, you may downright offend a quick-to-anger spirit—not fun!

Before embarking on a trance journey, it is a good and wise idea to possess a mind map of the world/s you are about to enter, at least mentally or theoretically. Understand, however, that trance propels consciousness into the regions between and beyond what is decidedly "normal," and as such trancers will often find themselves floundering around in the astral for a moment or two. If you are working through a cultural tradition such as the Norse, and you intend to scale the world tree Yggdrasil, then please account for the realms you may pass through on your way to Valhalla, as well as the laws. As with anything in Neopaganism, if spirituality is to be placed within a cultural context, then respect, at all times, must be the law: respect the ancient traditions and customs that infuse the worldview of the peoples whom you are evoking as ethnic or spiritual ancestors.

Ritualistically speaking, to entrance oneself and facilitate a journey, there are countless methods and techniques that are able to arouse the consciousness to do just that. When I entrance, I tend to simply ground and centre as per usual, and then I focus on the void within and join that sacred truth with the greater void that permeates and underlies all things, and "as above, so below," I enter a trance state. There are myriad ways one can enhance the sensations of trance and in this way urge the conscious mind into accepting the reality of trance.[33] Once this boundary to success has been dissolved, trance becomes the non-ordinary reality, which gradually, over time, becomes quite ordinary, though without losing its innate magickal quality.

The Body-Rocking Technique

One of my earliest memories of entering a trance state was at the house altar in my childhood home, kneeling and rocking back and forth with my torso straight. The basis for this technique is the pendulum effect of inducing a hypnotic rhythm. The word *rhythm* comes from the ancient Greek *rhein,* meaning "to flow." When we have flow, we create a dynamic current that is at one with the current of the cosmos, and all we can do is "go with the flow," thus inducing trance.

Trance Dance

I have spoken about trance dance quite a few times in the length of this book; however (with no intention to appear repetitive), here the technique is again—in all its glory!

Simply turn on some favourite music (African drumming tracks tend to work well), and let go of all inhibition. Open to liberation, and

---

33 This works on the premise that today's human beings are decidedly materialistic and thus require physical sensations to confirm something as true or worthy of that consideration. I remember when my coven received its first students, and during one of our early circles, a girl exclaimed that in her many years of practising the Craft, our power-raising had been the first time she actually felt the energy. I could clearly see how that experience had impacted and strengthened her sense of involvement within the Craft.

claim your divine right to dance! If it helps your cause, dance the spirit of your totem animal or your patron deity, and through the mythos and archetype of your spirit ally, access hidden dimensions of power contained within the self. This is the aim of much trance, after all.

As you dance, feel the spinning vortex of reality swallow itself and be ready to jump into the void—take the risk, and place trust in your own keen endeavour to discover new vistas of being and understanding. Break through the outworn moulds and patterns of beliefs, and surrender as the undulations of the body propel you further into deep awareness of the All-Self; embrace…embrace…and let go!

The Herbal Trance Technique

For this trance technique, be prepared to work with our herbal friends. You will need a fireproof container (e.g., a cauldron), a good charcoal disc, a mortar and pestle, and a combination of trance-inducing herbs, e.g., mugwort, rue, and wormwood. Ground and centre, and with the pestle, begin to crush and grind up the herbs together in the mortar. As you do, make sure you name and bless each of the herbs by name and quality. For instance, if the herb is mugwort, say something like: "Mugwort, dreaming herb, I awaken thy spirit to inspire within me the power of the 'tween places. Blessed be." Light the charcoal disc and place it in the fireproof container; sprinkle the herbs onto the disc and sit/stand comfortably within range of the rising smoke. Breathe in the smoke, and let it intoxicate your being. As the smoke spirals and dissipates into the atmosphere, allow the ego to dissolve and join in oneness with the All-Self.

You can also integrate herbal help into your trance techniques through the use of essential oils (anointing) and even through tea infusions (steeping herbs in boiled water). As always, approach each herb in the shamanic manner—name the herb, entitle the herb with an epithet, list the qualities, and bless the herb.

You will know when you have become entranced, as the following qualities and emotions are sure to be exhibited and experienced:

- Total oneness and connectedness with the All-Self
- The blurring of boundaries
- Liberation and freedom (the loss of inhibitions)
- Unconditional love
- Bliss and ecstasy
- Touching the Divine (the core)

TꞭE POWER OF TRANCE

Most people who experience trance states agree that they
are accompanied by a feeling of great well-being. No matter
what the exact nature of the experience may be, this response
is almost always recognizable and is the product of an
increased awareness of being at one with Creation.
—John Matthews, *The Celtic Shaman: A Handbook*

I have already dealt with the decidedly more objective and methodical parts above; however, trance is more than what can be viewed and spoken about at a safe, cold distance. To experience the power of trance, one must dive into the deep end and subsume all awareness in the non-awareness of non-ordinary reality. We must learn that most difficult of lessons: we are not always in control. Remember that to entrance, we must let go and let the gods.

Try this: create a large enough space for you to move and dance around in without hurting yourself or tripping over anything. Open all the windows, light some of your favourite incense and candles, and play music that you can't help but lose it to. Ground and centre, and don't try too hard in terms of feeling, sensing, raising, channeling, directing, and releasing power; this is not meant to be a ceremonial rite, although it bears the same holy significance.

Just dance! Open yourself to freedom! Leap, twirl, salsa, and dip to the rhythm that is inspired in your body by each wave of musically charged magick as it hits you. *Dance! Dance! Dance!* You could easily transport this example in exercising personal freedom and power to be and thrive into a nightclub, drumming circle, or—if you're game enough—to the middle of the street! I'm sure, like me, you sometimes wish that life could be one big musical. Trance can really be that simple...and exciting!

Recently, at a Pagan gathering, I held a workshop that I entitled "Trance Dance." Before we got to the trancy bit, I led the group on a pathworking to meet our power animals, which we would trance dance in reverence of their wisdom and meaning. We had previously stretched and warmed up our bodies, so when the time came for the music (funky beats indeed!), we were ready and raring to go! We held hands, and as the beat increased in tempo, I encouraged people to relax into the rhythm and let their bodies feel and receive the inspiration of the flow in the moment. We began to spiral dance, and the heat in the room rocketed! In and out, in and out, and then...*Go! Be free! Dance your animal! Make them proud!* The participants outdid themselves, and they certainly made their power animals proud. The energy in that room was vital, raw, and bursting at the seams with passion. The power of trance is the power of release, the potency of freedom, and the lesson of *now*!

In the same breath, trance is also a powerful medium through which to commune with the spirit world, facilitate drawing down/possession, and make real the mantle of the oracle. Trance is both an altered state of consciousness (a state of being and of perception) and a method through which to attain such states. Trance is an incredible and vast powerhouse, and if approached with respect and integrity, one can awaken the mysteries and draw near the threshold of initiation. Trance propels seekers into the otherworlds. Seek and dare.

I will end this chapter by relaying the last official aspirant training session I facilitated with a beloved friend who is now an initiated priestess of the Coven of the WildWood.

Becky and I met in the city and followed tradition by indulging in blessed bubble tea, followed by delicious sushi. I will preface the rest of this brief foray into the training and teaching world of WildWood by explaining that Becky herself was an interesting case, in terms of aspiration and as a student of the Craft. Becky had been initiated as a first-degree priestess of a Celtic-Avalonian tradition several years before she decided to aspire to WildWood. Becky lives her Craft and is a very experienced and profoundly insightful Witch—in a nutshell, she's good at what she does. Thus, her aspirant training was an interesting case in point. Many times we simply had what we in priesthood training call "fat (phat) chats," in which we simply divulge our opinions, feelings, experiences, and insights about _____ (insert aspect of Craft/Pagan spirituality here).

Becky and I were walking through the shoe section of Myer fat-chatting about trance and what it means. We spoke of trance as a means to attain other states of consciousness, or being, which can help facilitate:

- Spirit flight and journeying into other realms
- Drawing down (or in) gods and other appropriate spiritual beings
- Channeling information and wisdom from various sources (mediumship or oracular work)

The "lesson," in contrast with the previous sessions, however, was decidedly more lax, and I found myself dissatisfied. On the bus home after finishing up in the city, I realised that we had definitely covered the practical aspects and exercises associated with trance throughout her four months of weekly training. I had helped Becky to successfully draw down our Crescent-Crowned Goddess, fly to and through other realms, and transport her consciousness to become one with the ever-spiralling mythos of the WildWood. Leaving the city that afternoon was rather emotional for me, as Becky and I had grown so close and developed such a strong friendship during that time that we both agreed we would continue with our weekly one-on-one get-togethers, despite the "official" completion of her aspirant training (and we still call it aspirant training, just for fun). I decided it was right and fitting that I send her a message to express my feelings and also to conclude the lesson on trance:

> *Thank you so much for the friendship that has grown between us through this whole process. I absolutely love you, and if you decide to dedicate, it will affirm to me that you have been, are, and always will be my sister. In my mind, you are already so much a part of it... Trance is the way we feel when we have become intoxicated with life's essence, when we have dissolved the boundaries between the conscious and the unconscious, and are at one with the All-Self, which is at the core of our being. Thou art Goddess!*

That afternoon, I decided that trance leads to the gnosis of self through awareness of the All-Self. The barriers that we perceive to exist between what is considered "self" and what is seen to be "not-self" dissolve in the face of the being that has, in the very Islamic sense of the word, surrendered to the All. Muslims might contextualise this philosophy as one of complete surrender to Allah, the merciful creator, sustainer, and cherisher of the worlds. A Pagan might simply say, "Go with the flow."

Trance leads to altered states of consciousness that facilitate an awakening of the true, essential self that exists at our deepest layer. In my humble twenty-one years in this incarnation, I have experienced trance states while dancing in clubs, making love, walking, riding the bus, and certainly while meditating in circle. Trance is that paradoxical process and entirely human force that simultaneously elevates, contracts, tears apart, and expands. It is that primal cauldron (symbol of the mystery) in which Dionysos was boiled and eventually restored by the ancient Earth Mother herself to greater glory. Dionysos awakens to his true self and finds that "self" is in all things—as above, so below; as within, so without. All is a mirror! All is one!

12

TO JOURNEY AND VISION

As she and several other medicine people had emphasized
to me, the quest was not primarily about deprivation
but about seeking insight for oneself and others.
—Marie Herbert, *Healing Quest*

In various shamanic traditions the world over, themes of oracular
vision journeys crop up time and time again. In fact, these spirit journeys often parallel modern occult preambles concerning astral travel
or projection. This chapter will not discuss astral journeying, as it has
been covered already (see chapter 8, "To Fly in Spirit"); however, the
deepening of awareness and the vision-journey techniques of ages and
cultures past will be regarded in detail.

GAIA, FREYA, AND APOLLON—OH MY!
Seership in the ancient oracular sense was revered by the Old Ones.
It manifested under various guises in different cultures globally; how-
ever, it all seems to stem from the same understanding of the cosmos

and the same human yearning to have insight into the "wyrding web," or the tide of fate.

In ancient Greece, the most famous oracular tradition was that of the Delphic oracle. Delphi was believed in ancient times to be the *omphalos*, or the navel/centre of the world itself. The mytho-history of the Delphic oracle is rather obscure and possibly skewed by an Indo-European/Kurgan invasion, which eventually led to the supplantation of the goddesses as the prime catalysts in myth and religion. The gods seized absolute power, a patriarchal goal. The myth of Delphi itself—and thus the oracle—is rather telling.

There are various legendary accounts that describe Delphi and its oracular powers. One myth in particular, however, has been upheld by Pagan and goddess-worshipping feminists to illustrate and support the historical theories of Marija Gimbutas, the late and notorious Lithuanian feminist historian and archaeologist who created the Kurgan hypothesis. The site of Delphi was once known as Pytho, which comes from a Greek root meaning "to rot," referring to the decomposition of the titanic bodies of Gaia's guardian serpents who dwelt there (Gaia being the Earth Mother from whom we all come and who was born from Kaos/Chaos). The decomposition of the serpents was inferred by Apollon, the new lord of prophecy, who slew the "monstrous" creature and claimed the oracular seat of power for himself. In other myths, it is said that Delphi and its powers were in the hands of the goddesses Themis and Phoebe, who at the coming of Apollon to Delphi wilfully handed the reigns of power to the god. Whatever the truth of the matter (though myth is never an objective thing), Delphi has been known for millennia to be the holy seat of oracular power— the centre of the world.

The Pythia—the oracle herself—and her wisdom (the words of the gods, Apollon, Gaia, or whomever) were the focus and the pinnacle of any visit to Delphi. Her words and oracles have been recorded through the sands of time by countless literary greats, including

Herodotus, Euripides, Aristotle, and Plato, though the authenticity of the psychic nature or divine origins of the channelings have often been scrutinised.

It has been hypothesised that the tripod the Pythia sat on when giving oracles stood over a fissure in the rocks through which gaseous fumes emanated, which possibly helped to induce the Pythia's deeply abiding trance. However, the attendant priests, who were entirely conscious during the proceedings, were the ones who "translated" the divine tongue ("gibberish") and framed the oracles for the seekers. Once again, this can be viewed as patriarchal providence, as it was the priests who delivered the divine ordains despite the actual oracles spouting from the lips of a female priestess. In fact, historically and in classical Greece, the position of the Delphic oracle was perhaps the single most significant and powerful role a woman could aspire towards. Originally, the oracle was said to be a young virgin; however, the law/lore changed to allow elderly women (even if married) to take on the mantle of Pythia, though upon becoming the Pythia, one had to renounce all family ties and dissolve personal identity.

Interestingly, the role of seer, at least in Europe, was often equated with mysterious feminine powers. In northern Europe and among the Nordic tribes, the oracular arts were entirely women's business. In *Northern Mysteries & Magick* (Llewellyn, 1998), Freya Aswynn states matter-of-factly that "in Old Norse, the name for a female magician was *volva*, which means 'sibyl' or 'prophetess.' Her main function was to practice divination." In Norse and other Germanic traditions, vision journeying is called spae-craft or seidr, which can generally be translated as meaning Witchcraft. Several Pagan reconstructionist groups in the Northern Hemisphere have re-created the old tribal ceremonies that enabled the seer/priestess/volva to enter trance and commune with the spirit world. The patron deity of this art is Freya—the Norse *vanir* (earth) goddess of sorcery/seidr, sexuality, love, and fertility.

Seidr magick works on the premise that the seidr worker "seeks to sink into the realm of the unknown and unconscious, to become woven into it."[34] In becoming "woven into" the web of Wyrd (the fabric of the cosmos and the reason for it), the mundane space-time continuum dissipates, and time instead becomes a river that flows, of course, to the sea, or the matrix. In this state of enhanced awareness (All-Self), one can pierce the veil of illusion and perceive truth. Through the facilitation of trance states, a practitioner of seidr magick is able to speak with the spirits, who are beings of raw potency and great wisdom, and learn of things long lost to the past, the hidden realties of the present, and those things that are still to come. This is possible because all time is time, and there is only what is now—now and now again.

Seidr, like all shamanic traditions, helps to alter consciousness and inspire ecstasy, propelling the self into the wonder of Wyrd. The intricate cosmology that informs and enlivens the rites and ceremonies of northern folk magicians helps to guide and align the modern-day seidr practitioner with the world tree—the joiner of all the worlds and thus the highway for vision journeying.

In spae-craft, the priestess is aided in her trance induction by her attendant seidr workers through the medium of song. The songs are sung as the volva eats a meal that was traditionally comprised of the hearts of wild creatures. She then climbs onto a platform and seats herself on a high chair; she is dressed in a feathered cloak and catskin gloves. These vestments are worn in honour of the goddess Freya, to whom these rites are dedicated. Once the trance state is attained, the priestess then begins to prophesy; her information comes directly from the spirit world in which she dwells for a time. The parallels between seidr and the Delphic oracle are obvious; however, the feminine expertise associated with visionary powers is highlighted in the northern example. Perhaps in the time that Delphi was considered

---

34 Edred Thorsson, *Northern Magic: Rune Mysteries and Shamanism* (Llewellyn, 2002), 16–17.

Gaia's sacred centre, the oracular rites were celebrated and directed by women.

The oracular deities share something subtle in common: their connection to the deeper chthonic mysteries. Gaia, whom Delphi was first dedicated to, contains within herself the various layers and realms of Hades, or the underworld. Freya, a Vanir goddess of fertility, forest, and field, is also the patron of seidr, which, according to Edred Thorsson, is a kind of "Northern shamanism." Any deity associated with the fertility of the earth is automatically connected to the chthonic powers, as all fertility first begins in the dark, moist womb of the earth. Apollon bears no obvious or particular underworldly connections; however, many myths and writings concerning Delphi state that Dionysos was the reigning lord of the Delphic oracle for the winter months, and this deity's strong chthonic aspects were highly honoured. Like the darkly nurtured seeds that become the summer's heavy-laden harvest, so too is the wisdom of the spirits gathered and kept in the subterranean realms until the enlightenment (Apollon's brilliant gold rays) of the mind strikes the fecund soil and draws them into the light of day. The journey to the underworld to retrieve and claim visions is an experience and technique of altering consciousness that I call "the journey across the sunless sea."

GOING UNDER: JOURNEYING ACROSS THE SUNLESS SEA

Life and death were a continuous stream; the dead were buried as if sleeping in a womb, surrounded by their tools and ornaments, so that they might awaken to a new life.
—Starhawk, *The Spiral Dance*

In vision journeying, one is required to disengage from the ego—from the independent, discrete identity—and dissolve into the oneness of the All-Self, which affirms the truths of interconnection, no-time, and no-space. Upon attaining such a state of consciousness, we are able to move freely between the worlds and access knowledge and wisdom from hidden realms.

Starhawk and the Reclaiming Collective of San Francisco use similar terminology when referring to the voyage of the souls of our beloved dead "beyond the sunless sea." I use a similar reflection because it is only through awareness of the "temporary-eternally-shifting-changing" nature of things that one is able to break free from paradigms of (or desire for) unnatural, unchanging, bodily immortality, which engenders a fear and hatred for and of death.

In the Craft traditions, Death is the king who initiates our queen, the Goddess, into the mysteries of rebirth (more on this later). It is only through death that we become what we always were and are—eternity ever-evolving. We are the dance of the Horned One who lives, dies, and is reborn.

"Going under" further qualifies my allusion to the realms of death, the underworld, the cauldron of regeneration, and the Celtic sea; thus is this section so named. Here is a rich pathworking that will lead you into the crucible of change and bring you to the very edge of life itself.

Voyage Across the Sunless Sea: Pathworking

Begin by grounding and centring yourself and creating sacred space in your own way. As trance/vision-journey incense, burn cypress, rosemary, and sage in equal parts on a charcoal disc.

Visualise yourself standing on the shoreline. Place yourself firmly in that reality of salty sea air, sea foam, sinking sand beneath your feet, and a lapping tide. Feel the foundation of the sand beneath you—this is the land. Feel the coolness of the water rushing around you—this is the sea. Look up into the heavens, and relax as the winds stir you—this is the sky. In this 'tween place, you are on holy ground, joined and blessed by the wholeness of the three realms. You are at one with the ancient trinity.

A mist gathers around you, and it feels as though a heavy grey cloak has settled over your shoulders. You breathe in and out, and the mist spirals and undulates, making strange, otherworldly patterns in the space before you. You feel the urge to step through the veil of mist, for there is a magnetic pull drawing you forward. Before you can take your first step into the unknown, the prow of a boat cuts out of the enfolding mist and a radiant, ethereal hand reaches out from beyond, coaxing you forward, onto the boat itself. Do you dare to travel across the sunless sea into the great beyond?

You dare to, and you will it; you take the proffered hand and feel the swift but sure strength of your guide as you are lifted into the boat. Now you come face to face with the being who would aid you. Allow time now to become acquainted with one another, although there is a great chance you already know each other.

The boat sails through the mist, navigating itself intuitively upon the waves and through the veils of time and space, as you have come to know the mists. You feel as if you are being transported to another place, another time, outside of space and time. Your guide assures you that all will be well and that a purpose underlies this voyage. In your heart, you are deeply aware of the purpose that has inspired this journey.

There is a faint red glow in the distance, on what your guide tells you is the western horizon. You suddenly realise that somehow you didn't notice the light of the sun travelling the arc of the sky to finally set in the west, but your guide whispers to you that the sun never rises over this sea and neither does it set, for you are sailing the sunless sea to the great beyond. The sun's red glow is a constant of the western horizon in this realm—it is a continuing symbol of everlasting life, of certain rebirth, for nothing ever truly dies. Death is but a door.

Further and further the boat sails until the veils of time and space—the mists—become all-encompassing and take on a deep indigo hue. You have arrived at the fated Gate of Death—the threshold into the otherworld. The bow of the boat is halted by the power of he who guards the gate—the wolf god of the ancients. You bow, as does your guide, and the wolf god smiles, bearing his gleaming, sharp canine teeth. Your guide whispers a farewell to you, smiles, and disappears; this is a journey only you can make.

You stand alone at the prow of the boat and stare evenly into the dark, endless eyes of the primal wolf god before you. You see a demand in his eyes, and you feel ready and willing to meet this demand. You breathe in deeply, and all the courage of the world flows through you. You say,

> I, (state your name), upon the waves of the sunless sea that
> I have journeyed across to meet with you, acknowledge you,
> Wolf God, as the king of rest that grants rejuvenation,
> death granting new life, and the wisdom of these ancient
> transitions, which have been and will be forever. Blessed be.

The wolf god's eyes gleam wildly with a lusty excitement, and your gut is hit with a wave of anticipation; in the shortness of a moment, in the timelessness of this no-place, all becomes dark, and you feel and know that you are no longer in the realm of the living or upon the sunless sea. You have crossed through the indigo veil and arrived in the place of death. You expect fear, and yet you are filled with a sense of boundlessness and freedom. The darkness becomes lighter as the spirit within you quivers and relaxes itself into the great unknown. The mystery has alighted!

RETRIEVING VISIONS FROM THE WELL OF MEMORY

It is terrible how much has been forgotten, which is why, I suppose,
remembering seems a holy thing...I will pour out everything
inside me so you may leave this table satisfied and fortified.
—Anita Diamant, *The Red Tent* (Dinah's words)

In ancient Greek myth, a detailed description of Hades (the underworld) can be found in many literary and visual sources. A common factor in almost every detailing of Hade's realm is the River of Lethe—the river of forgetfulness. According to one Orphic myth, beside the spring/river of Lethe is a white cypress; the Orphics warned against drinking from this spring, as they held an implicit belief in reincarnation and were conscious mystics pursuing an ecstasy-driven path of pious worship for the Divine within all things, including each other. By the Lake of Memory is another spring which is guarded. The ritual instructions to allow passage to the bank of the Lake of Memory to drink are given as follows (and must be spoken to the beings guarding the lake):

> I am child of earth and of starry heaven, but my race is of heaven alone. This ye know yourselves. And lo, I am parched with thirst and I perish. Give me quickly the cool water flowing from the Lake of Memory.[35]

Upon such ceremonial utterance, the guards are said to submit to one's will to drink and allow passage through to the lake.

In the various Pagan shamanic traditions, the "well/lake of memory" is noted clearly in the associated cosmologies. For example, at the base of the Nordic world tree Yggdrasil lies the Well of Memory, which nourishes the roots that coil around the Wyrd waters.

---

35 Translated from unearthed Orphic gold-leaf texts (dating from as early as the seventh century BCE and as late as the second century CE).

In *Exploring the Northern Tradition* by Galina Krasskova, the author gives an insight into the interconnectivity of the mighty tree Yggdrasil:

> *Yggdrasil supports the web of fate, woven by the Nornir, three wise women that oversee the Well and use its sacred waters to nourish the Tree…Yggdrasil has three mighty tap roots, each extending into one manifestation of the sacred well: one terminates in Niflheim, into the well Hvergelmir; one in Jotunheim, into the well of Memory, the well of the Jotun Mimir; and one into Urdabrunnr, the well of fate.*[36]

The author goes on to explain how the dragon Nidhoggr is constantly gnawing at the roots of the tree, which would eventually destroy all the worlds and plunge all into the abyss. However, the three Norns tend to the inflicted wounds on the tree's roots by nourishing them with the sacred waters of Urda's well and restoring the cosmic balance. This cultural insight into the ancient Pagan cosmology—and way of thinking (and of life)—reflects the significance of the symbolism of memory in the magickal traditions.

When we as Witches journey and quest for visions, we enter the fabric by which is spun the stuff of the worlds, and thus we are swallowed into the unconscious realms of archetypes, symbols, raw forces, and mighty beings. The ancient realms are only sleeping, awaiting our keen interest to awaken and claim sovereignty of spirit once more. Knock on the door, and if you are of pure intent and trust burns brightly at the crest of your heart, you will be admitted into the otherworlds. Seek out the Well of Memory and drink from the cool waters of vitality, for these will sustain your soul and invigorate your mind.

Re-membering is a very powerful act. It means to sew together what once were many disparate pieces scattered to the cruel and bitter winds of disconnection and disharmony. Invoke harmony and weave

---

36 Page 31.

with the inherent connections, and you will be gifted with the ability to holistically heal what many people today experience as trauma, discomfort, loss, confusion, and apathy. These things are the products of a life lived separated from the vital flow that sustains our dreaming— what the Norse call "wyrd"—memory being remembered.

Many modern-day shamans are resurrecting the ancient practice of soul retrieval, which aims to help wounded beings restore the vital balance of wholeness—our birthright. Briefly, soul loss is said to happen when an individual is deeply affected by a sudden and traumatic incident (e.g., the death or loss of a loved one, or a personal near-death experience). A piece of soul is said to break away from the whole, and this fragment, in a very childlike manner, flees to what it deems a safe place. There it will remain until someone skilled in the area (a Witch, a shaman, a psychotherapist, etc.) is able to correctly diagnose this psychic circumstance and take the right steps towards retrieving the soul fragment and restoring the patient's wholeness. I witnessed soul loss rather strongly when a good friend of mine experienced the death of his brother.

My friend received the call on the day of the summer solstice. Our household was busily getting ready for the open ritual our coven was holding that day to celebrate Litha. My friend quietly explained to us that his brother had passed away the night before in a car accident, but he insisted that we continue with the ritual and that he would be present; he was to draw in our god of the waning year, the wolf god, who would battle and triumph over our lord of the waxing year, the stag king. The following two months we watched as our friend sunk into a deeper and deeper haze; I observed many times the fluttering of a frightened, shocked, and bruised soul within him. I was at a loss at what to do. My friend was in mourning and despair, but there were no avenues of expression and no context in which to place the loss of his beloved brother. Life and death—these things make up our wheel. It is a hard lesson to learn.

One evening as I showered and entered into the WildWood (the astral realm/counterpart of the original WildWood, which is by nature all that was/is wild and free on this planet), as I am sometimes prone to do as part of cleansing, I saw that my friend's various totems were moving around, looking lost and dull. Everything slid neatly into place in that moment, and I realised then that this was a case of soul loss. I explained this to my friend one afternoon, and we embraced as he cried and nodded and expressed that he was unsure of what to do. I told him that I would help, and we organised a time for a ritual I hoped would facilitate the necessary soul retrieval.

The afternoon came, and we set up our circle. We had spoken during the week of the ritual, and in that time I had several powerful experiences with the goddesses Isis (Auset) and Persephone (my soul goddess). I thought it would be a great idea if we could invoke a different goddess of healing and shamanic transformative magick at every quarter and for the centre as well. In the east we called upon Isis (the air), in the north we called upon Tara (the fire), in the west we called upon Persephone (the water), and in the south we called upon Freya (the earth). In the centre we called upon our beloved Crescent-Crowned Goddess of the WildWood, who represents the journey for and of love into the realm of darkness and once more into the bright realm of the living—the deity many Witches call simply "the Goddess."

I had intended the goddesses' presences to be a helpful facilitation for my own revitalising and holistic healing work on my friend; however, as should be expected, they had something else in mind. After we had formed and consecrated our space in the name of our work and in the presence of the goddesses, I felt the impulse to go to each quarter and channel wisdom from each of them; instead, each goddess decided to entirely possess me (hand in glove) and share communion with my friend in this way. As per usual, the memories of this drawing-down experience are vague and, if thought about, slip away like water in cupped hands; my friend relayed much of what was said and imparted to him. Each goddess, in their divine wisdom, helped to break down the emotional barriers and walls that had developed since his brother's death. Each one had aided him in a self-transformation that culminated in our beloved Lady of the Moon bringing him to the sword of initiation once more and demanding that he, without fear, take up the charge and live! I came out of my reverie to see bright eyes and a wide smile on an old friend's revivified face.

I saw clearly the enormous change that had taken place in him during that circle. Also, during this sacred communion, a storm had appeared out of nowhere in the east and travelled deosil as each goddess in turn spoke around the circle and whirled around our house, only to clear as the goddesses withdrew their power and presence and the circle was opened. The goddesses' message was this:

> *Nothing true and essential can ever be lost. You are always whole—you must always remember this holy truth, in every day, in every moment. Hold true to truth, and wholeness will be a gift of the gods. Happiness will ever follow those who walk the path of the Divine. You and your soul's dancing fragments are but the endless waves of the sea who is the over-flowing grail of that mysterious force we call love. Be well and wise, our blessed child.*

13

TO CHANNEL

If you step into the Beyond, the full force of
Nature shall pivot in your being.
—Michael J. Roads, *Journey into Nature*

MEDIUMSHIP:
ON BEING AN ORACLE

I have decided, as Witches tend to do (with zest, fervour, and smiling faces), to channel advice, wisdom, and truth regarding channeling for this chapter. As I started to write this chapter, it came upon me that the universe should have a say. I hope you, the reader, enjoy this diversion.

The Channeling

[1] Like waves upon the sea, the foamy crest of the heaving ocean we call Mother are we. Each of us aligned according to our inner rhythm and innate sense of wonder and being, and thus we are perfected upon the shores of the timeless ones. Like a cell within a larger body, a wave is unto the greater ocean—the

sameness and oneness that pervades the entirety dwells within the consciousness of the wave. The wave holds within itself the miraculous, all-encompassing infinity that is the ocean.

[2] A human channel, or vessel, is much the same. Within each of us resides the endless sanctuaries of collected knowledge and wisdom, and thus by our innate interconnection and divine unity, we are able to access this powerhouse of insight and cosmic knowing. When we channel, we open ourselves to the undivided awareness of the illumined whole and we ourselves become privy to the subtlest of mysteries.

[3] As I type this, I have ignited within myself the capacity of "channel." I have become a vessel and a conduit through which the blessed beauty of the words of the immortals may resonate and flow. My audience in no way compares to the intimate gatherings of Witches or lay-folk who approach the oracle of the gods with reverence and, without knowing why, intrinsic fear. However, there is no need to fear what is true—and what is true is simply what is. Ultimately it is up to the perceiver of truth to know it and align with it, or to cast it aside and wish for blind insanity instead. I am of you, as you are of me. Truth is one, though it sings in the veins of a diverse creativity—the truth you know, though it is my truth also, will appear differently to you. Understanding this, we honour the sacred and its desire and yearning to know itself and hold the communion of love.

[4] Let the words of the gods flow through me. Let these lips become a sacrament to the breath-propelled key to the mysteries. Let these fingers become the wands of a thousand wizards as they cast their sorcery into the frozen night. Know this, my friends: it is not within you that you shall find the answer to what lies beyond…beyond is more than ego. Beyond is the illustrious counterpart that destroys the illusion of separation. When you discover what is beyond, you are brought to the knees of salva-

tion, and through it we are initiated into selfhood. We become what we are, and we realise we are one with the holy of holies and we are wholly divine.

[5] It is not without merit to seek what is beyond within, for the truth lies in the heart of all things. As "I" exist, so do "you." The "I" seems permeable, in a sense, for what is I can also be what is the I that is you. If identity is sacrosanct in the universal sense, then all who proclaim in zealous, wild abandon that "I am I" will feel the underlying profundity of what is "I." Many centuries ago, before a burning bush and on a holy mountain, did a young tribal god proclaim to his prophet, "I am that I am." I am, and without the I, the am is an empty mirror. The I beholds the mirror and the reflection, and thus creation is born in the guise of what was not there before the I was perceived. All flow, one from the next, in simple and starving yearning, both together and both apart, like two serpents entwining upon the rod carved from the tree of life, which grows in paradise. These images may seem to you whatever they instill; however, the point of the images is to unite across the breadth of culture and nation. I am the Spirit who says that beside the nation and the identity is the Am. I AM.

[6] In this wild state of arousal, so is the Spirit said to move from base to crown and awaken the mighty power of what is within—what lies beyond. When the Spirit ignites at the crown, let the flame burn brightly, for it is a beacon to all those which flow with the tide of nature. I am (you are, we are) the rhythm that inspires the tides and allows it to continue in its cycle of ways. In the morning I am the dawn, at the high noon of day I am the sun at its peak, and in the time of sunset I am the merging of colours long forgotten as the paints of the heavenly artists are spilled and the ego is obliterated beyond the horizon. I am midnight—the stillness of darkness and the womb of the earth that generates all life upon this the green planet of blue.

[7] Hold within the seat of your awareness the oneness that is all-pervasive and that joins the hearts of the many nations to beat as one. I am the light of the world, and I am the darkness of the moist and sweet earth, the crucible of creation. You cannot have one without the other, and it is through the two united that the third is engendered, and so the cycle is sewn into the very fabric of being. And so it was, and so it is, and so it shall forever be. The third is eternal. Take upon yourself the mantle of the third, and wear over your crown the veil of the most holy.

[8] My wings are the wings of the heavenly messengers, the angels who bear the voices of the manifold winds. Let the peace of those who serve bring surrender to the souls who yearn for the "I am." In the stillness that is oneness and the movement that is celebration, may all be joined in the song of reverence that causes the knee to bend and the hand to upturn. Let our cups be full of the wine of life, and let the merriment of the day lead to the mystery of the night. One from the next, ever-turning and seeking to inspire.

[9] This is the message of what kneels at the foot of the immortal chamber and sings sweetly within the blood-rivers that wind through the body of God. Gnosis—awaken! I am what is slumbering, and what is rising, and what is eternally so. Let it be—as the Mother honours the silence, so you shall, to honour the Mother.

[10] Upon the ancient seat, upon the litter of the spirits, place yourself, and open your mouth to the breath of the Divine. Let the ancients know through you and tell the story that is already a part of your understanding. Let life continue as you sing the songs and declare the secrets of the hidden ones to those who would have ears to listen and eyes to witness. But more than this, touch the hearts of those who yearn to be touched, for they are humble in their ways and in their desire to please. Let them not

prostrate unless they do so in the spirit of complete and total surrender—that is the spirit which causes the rain to fall and the earth to bring forth the bounty of summer. Speak with lips anointed by the sacred words that are yours to speak. The torch that is yours to bear will ignite before you and inspire the wind as it flows through your mouth and brings sound to the assemblies—the children of earth and of heaven.

[11] Let this be known, and let there be the kneeling, and let there be the standing, and the silence and the sound, and the bridge in between. Thou art the bridge that has been formed and forged and resurrected to serve the purpose of channel. Become the river of that Mighty One who causes the seas to swell and the stars to pierce the veil of the heavens. Be unto yourself in that timelessness of space, and let there be forever peace within thee—let the fire burn bright. And know this simple, humble nature of what is borne by the angels who, as we know, are the servants of those who are the servants of the mystery...to serve is to surrender to the knowing, to the truth. The beyond is the river that winds its way through the body of you and carries the life-blood to the heart, which beats in yearning to meet and marry with what is beyond. Say to yourself "I am," and you will understand the meaning of my words, and I will say to you, "I am," and we will have come to that most ancient of places, to that most holy of times: forever.

TḥE INTERPRETATION

Before I attempt to communicate my interpretation of the above channelled message, I would like to say that, in my experience, what I call channeling is always done in a state of self-consciousness. However, the art of channeling also tends to entrance the individual who is performing the part of the conduit, or channel, and thus the state of being one finds oneself in during these sessions can be quite hard to describe, somewhat like lucid dreaming. For instance, as I channelled the above for the purposes of this chapter, I discovered that I was still able to type in my swift speed and yet I was also somewhat transported into a blessed timelessness that carried the quality of forever, just as is described in the channeling. I was also quite delighted in the outcome, as I had never attempted, on such a scale, to channel and record by writing a message from the cosmos. I procrastinated quite a lot in regard to fulfilling the destiny of this chapter, as I was uncertain how my plans would manifest. Fortunately, and I feel quite blessed for it, all unfolded as it should, and voilà! This chapter came fully fleshed into being before my very eyes.

I will deal with the channeling paragraph by paragraph and garner meaning from each in turn. I approached this channeling session with the intent to draw from the cosmos and the immortal gods' wisdom and counsel on the meaning, purpose, and process of the craft of channeling—the mediumship of the oracle.

In paragraph 1, the message is clear—what is self is synonymous with what is All-Self. This has been a common theme and message throughout this entire book. It is a shamanic truth! It is the wisdom derived from experiences of sacred gnosis. In my book *Spirited,* I lend a whole section in my Divinity chapter to the Upanishadic philosophy of ancient Vedic India, which taught this awareness as atman (soul)-Atman (Spirit)—soul to Spirit, or Brahman. This, then, is the sacred knowledge required for success in channeling.

In paragraph 2, the message of oneness and divine unity is reiterated, except this time with specific association accorded to the art and practice of channeling. The images evoked speak of sanctuaries of knowledge and the like. The message seems to describe channeling as a way of "plugging in" to the dynamic wholeness of the cosmos and therefore acquiring the key to the mysteries—to all the knowledge and wisdom that exists eternally.

Paragraph 3 brings the attention to those who gather to hear the oracles and the messages channelled from the Divine. The channeling brings up what it calls "intrinsic fear," which I take to mean that child-like fear and rejection of the unknown that permeates all humanity. The message is clear once more: do not deny truth, and do not fear or abhor it. Accept truth, as it is truth, but understand that because we are manifold and diverse (and this is the nature of existence), truth will manifest to each of us differently—in a guise we each will uniquely embrace and yearn for. In this paragraph, the dynamic nature of creation is also mentioned, and many Witches and Pagans will recognise the wisdom contained within the last sentence—the life force (or whatever you call it) chooses to diversify because it wishes for the joy and desire found in the communion of lovers, which can only be inspired by initial separation. See the Feri tradition's writings (including Starhawk's) on creation to understand the insight and to engage with the beautiful poetry.

Paragraph 4 ultimately speaks of divine wholeness (we're all in it together as one); however, it initiates this by encouraging the individual to look beyond the ego into the "beyond"—the bigger picture, or what is more than the sum of its parts. I take this as "look only at difference if, when you do, you can see the unity that joins all things." When we truly understand this sacred truth, we are initiated into the mystery and we become one—we are enlightened.

In paragraph 5, the underlying theme of the oneness of things is continued; however, in this paragraph, the sacred "I"—the universal identity—is proclaimed as being of great value when we understand that the "I" is the common factor, or quality, that unites us all. We can each attest to being "I," and thus is "I" a sacred expression of being, especially when it is contextualised by "am." The channeling then goes on to give what I assume is a biblical reference to Moses discovering Yahweh (the "young tribal god") in the burning bush on the mountain, and the deity describes himself as "I am that I am." However, the deep teaching here is that in the case of "I am," it is the "I" that gives form to the "am," for the "am" is preexistent, as existence can only exist when there is "I"—the sacred identity of what exists—to make it so. However, the I alone cannot exist unless the "am" generates or lends force and therefore birth to what can claim or identify "I." Interestingly, as I was re-reading the channelled message and particularly paragraph 5, I realised that in regard to the whole "I am" business, I felt a sudden mental linguistic paralleling; the English word "am" actually reminds me a lot of the Sanskrit "Aum"—the universal sound of all existence. There may be no historical or linguistic connections whatsoever; however, I have decided to make that intriguing connection here.

Paragraph 6 seems to be describing the rising of the Kundalini (serpent) energy from the base/root chakra to the crown, which many Hindu sages say can bring enlightenment. It seems that in this case perhaps it is true. Once again, the message relayed is that of divine unity between all things—all are cells (possessing the same DNA and concentration of life force) within the great body of life. The deepest within is the farthest beyond. There seem to be quantum parallels being drawn here (see page 59 for information on quantum physics). Regarding the rising serpent power through the body, the message seems to be suggesting that this energetically occurs during channeling and that when the power reaches the crown, it is a beacon to the spirits who "flow with the tide of nature." I would interpret this to mean those spirits which are of "the Good" in the Platonic sense. In terms of channeling, this is beneficial in that the aid of spirits external to the ego, or the "I" quality, of the human channel provides great leverage when it comes to acquiring and delivering messages. If the flame that ignites at the crown of the conduit draws in only benevolent spirits, then this is great news!

Paragraph 6 carries on to say that each of us are emissaries of the tide of nature and poetically identifies the individual consciousness with the four daily stations of the sun (i.e., sunrise, noon, sunset, and midnight). Briefly, if we equate childhood, adolescence, adulthood, and elderhood with dawn, noon, sunset, and midnight respectively, a pattern of developing consciousness can be imagined. At dawn we awaken to the first stirrings of consciousness; at high noon we discover the "I" in the "am." At the setting of the sun, our selfhood is invested in the care and attention of others to whom we wish to bear patronage, and in the silence of midnight we are brought to the heart of the Mother and bear the ancient gift of wisdom. It is this cycle that must be woven as living, breathing, evolutionary consciousness and as a way of mentally and psychically aligning while preparing oneself to be a channel.

In paragraph 7, the message speaks of the "light of the world" and the earth (moist and sweet). The words almost carry an undertone of Christ, and in a sense I can understand how many Wiccans would interpret this (and rightly so) to refer to the god of the sun and the earth mother (the God and the Goddess theology—Wiccan ditheism). However, the "third" is what is brought forth between the two, and this is the mantle of the most holy—the great mystery. We are all "third" (what equalises and balances, affirms and destroys [the illusion of] the two), as we came from the biological union of sperm and egg (father and mother). When channeling, focus on this simple fact—that we are all children who have been born of a lineage that never began in a time-continuum sense—we simply are and will continue to be. We are worthy of the Divine, for it is our birthright and our birth origin.

Paragraph 8 seems to indicate that when channeling we must begin with the peace which is instilled by the very process of becoming at one with the all-pervasive divine unity. After this, the expression, or way of communicating a divine message through channeling, can either be done in silence and stillness or through movement and revelry! Whatever part of the spectrum of human emotion best illustrates the point should definitely be used, and wholeheartedly so! Let there also be joy and peace in the hearts of those who have gathered to receive the wisdom, and let there be celebration in honour of the great Divine. The message conveyed in the last sentence of this paragraph, in my opinion, is that we should always aim to be open to inspiration, because to have the spirit within (in-spired)[37] is to be touched by truth, and this is a holy communion that brings many blessings.

Paragraph 9 begins the finalising of the "statement" of channeling. The spirit that has inspired the message is describing itself through poetic image and feeling, but in terms of the art of channeling, it seems that we have reached the part of the process in which the message has already been delivered and received, and silence and rest is now the key for the channel. This is the way of the Mother, and thus to honour her and invite her comfort, we are to honour her wish for silence. It is interesting that the phrase "let it be" is used in relation to a Divine Mother, for it brings to mind the Beatles' song "Let It Be" and the reference to Mother Mary (or a mother named Mary) nurturing the lost and troubled and speaking her wisdom.

In paragraph 10, the summation of the process of channeling is given so as to assert it within the mind of the beholder of the message. In fact, there are even suggestions as to how to place oneself physically to bear forth the messages of the Divine. When delivering the message of the gods, it is essential to speak in one's sense of knowing and understanding the world, as it is much easier for a human to understand and draw meaning from another human, as we are of similar experience. The next part of the paragraph seems to present advice on the practicality of channeling and drawing a crowd to listen and bear witness to the message. Let the world continue in its business around you as you bring forth the wisdom of the immortals, as there is no point in stopping the ways of all things simply to bring complete

37 Similar to "en-thused"—to have the Divine within.

focus to one human channel communicating with the Divine. This can be done in all times and in all places, and life can continue. The sacred is everywhere, and it is only where we place our minds and our hearts that determines whether or not we can truly experience the world as such. Also, in terms of those who gather, the channeling seems to suggest that only in the spirit of complete surrender (in the Islamic sense of the word) can we all share sacred time and space for such an event. This spirit of surrender is the spirit that flows with the tide of nature, as explained previously. The words that are the channel's to speak will be made obvious, as the "torch" (the inspiration) will guide the way. Merely allow the words, which will already be there, to cross from the unheard into the heard. Be the bridge between the worlds—this is the job of the channel, to join the heavens with the earth, and we are children of both.

And as for paragraph 11, I feel no point in expanding on what is already so forthrightly and evocatively said. I would simply have to suggest that you re-read it again and again, for there is more in those words than directions and advice on how to (be a) channel.

The Summation

It wouldn't hurt to summarise the key points of my interpretation of the channelled message on channeling to extract a comprehensive method to do just that:

- Centre and understand that self is Self (you are aligned and synonymous with the Great Being of the cosmos— the All-Self that is all-encompassing, all-pervasive, and underlying everything).

- Breathe in the divine unity that allows and provides access into the hidden realms of ancient knowledge and wisdom. Open to this power current and be at peace with the oneness that makes this possible.

- Prepare for truth and its multifaceted nature. Do not fear truth, for it is truth. Receive truth uniquely, and let others do the same.

- Go beyond the ego and embrace the beyond (the bigger picture), which can be found in the deepest part of the self.

- Repeatedly chant "I am," either inwardly or aloud, until it becomes one resounding "Aum." Let the repetition of the chant transform your consciousness.

- Allow the serpentine Kundalini force to rise, if it wills, from the base chakra to the crown, and allow a light to shine forth as a beacon to the benevolent spirits that would only seek to aid you and yours beneficially. Keep this intent pure and clear in your mind. As the Kundalini rises, feel it cleansing your energetic bodies and preparing your spirit for the flow of divine knowledge and wisdom.

- Visualise and focus momentarily on the four daily stations of the sun (sunrise, noon, sunset, and midnight), and allow your consciousness to evolve with the energy that is carried by each station. When you see the sunrise (in your mind's eye), feel the freshness and innocence of youth. When you see the noonday sun blazing brightly, feel the peak of vitality coming into, affirming, and celebrating your unique identity. When you see the sun setting over the horizon, feel the journey into deeper mysteries. When you envision what the midnight sun may look like buried deep within the womb of the Mother, honour the wisdom of the elders; it is at this point when you become ready to receive it.

- Now break the illusion of duality and become what balances and unites all things. Be the equaliser that inspires the profound silence of the observer. Be silent within but alert. You are the observer to what ensues. Be receptive. Affirm your divine worth within.

- Let the spirit move you while you convey the message as it should be conveyed. Move or be still…whatever emotion wishes to surface and be heard, let it have the platform. You are a channel of what is required (or conjured) to be heard.

- After the channeling, rest and be at peace in silence.

14

TO DIE AND BE REBORN

THE DESCENT OF THE GODDESS

In death she reveals the way to her communion.
—Raven Grimassi, *Hereditary Witchcraft*

The main mythos that pervades traditional Witchcraft[38] is that of the descent of the Goddess. This myth has been popularised in the Neo-pagan community ever since the publication and distribution of the Gardnerian (British Traditional Witchcraft) "Legend."

The *Legend of the Descent of the Goddess* is what I call a woman-finding story. It concerns our beloved Lady of the Moon and her quest to deepen her understanding of the cycles of life. Our lord of death and dying initiates her in the underworld, and the Goddess takes on the mantle of the circle of rebirth. She becomes the prototype of the Witch figure herself.

The descent mythos is important because it is multi-layered and speaks, as good myths do, to the deep unconscious, stirring primal

---

38 Especially those traditions influenced by the Mediterranean and Aegean cultures.

archetypes within the human psyche. In the Wiccan descent myth, there can be found several cultural influences that weave together to present the legend as it is given in the Book of Shadows. There are Sumerian (Inanna) undertones—e.g., the Goddess must remove all signs and symbols of her sovereignty and power (her crown, her clothes, her jewellery). There are notions in the myth that could connect with the Norse goddess Freya—e.g., the necklace/circlet of rebirth (Brisingamen, won from the four dwarves of the elemental directions). There are also direct Mediterranean/Aegean references that are written about at length in Raven Grimassi's works on Stregheria (Italian Witchcraft). Whether or not Wicca's native land of Britain affected the oral story that presumably became the myth is questionable, however, in that there are no known uniquely British mytho-symbols within the descent mythos that cannot be reflected or embodied within any of the aforementioned cultural contributions.[39]

The cross-cultural descent mythos informs the initiatory rites and inner psyche of the Witch who wanders with purpose through the Wyrd-ways of the weaver's web (life). In fact, in the second degree of Wiccan initiation, the descent mythos is enacted dramatically by the initiate and the high priest/ess to arouse the theme of inner death, ultimate transformation, and descent into the darkness to face one's Shadow, and to integrate and accept it. This is part of the process the late Carl Jung called individuation.

The Goddess descends into the underworld and passes through the gate of death because she longs for the warmth and radiance of her son/lover/king—the Horned God of the Witches. In the WildWood Tradition, we know the Horned One as the two-faced/natured deity

---

39 There are far too many striking parallels between Wicca and ancient Mediterranean/Aegean practices to ignore. The most poignant, I feel, are the "hidden" names of the Triple Goddess and the Horned God in the early Wiccan traditions (Aradia and Cernunnos, respectively). Both were Italian/Etruscan god-forms. The Celtic and Italic cultures were not unknown to each other, and indeed there are several historical instances in which religious syncretism occurred (one strong example is the adoption of the Gaulish horse goddess Epona by the Roman cavalry).

of Wolf and Stag; darkness and light, waning and waxing, day and night. He is our beloved lord of ecstasy, revelry, and expansion, and he is also the harbinger of decay, the primal exhilaration of the hunt (the dynamic dance of hunger, lust, and fear between the hunter and the hunted), and the old sage who beckons to the Witch seeking the threshold to initiation.

The Old Ones whisper, "If you are listening, you will learn." This is the force (the Horned One) the Goddess mourns; however, the Lady is momentarily suspended in disbelief that such a bright god of the sun, light, and the fulfilment of the harvest could also be the cold, wintry king of death and slumber.

The Goddess's initiation into the mysteries unfolds as the Lord of the Great Below (the other half to our bright and laughing upper-world king) teaches her of the necessity and generosity of the realm of death/rest in the grand scheme of things. He explains that those who have passed on may have respite before returning to the middle-world of challenge and hardship, though the choice to meet these tests with joy and mirth lies upon the being who is experiencing the earth-walk. The Goddess soon comes to understand the sovereignty and significance of death, and as the Dark Lord and Lady draw closer together in the winter cold, the two become intimately entwined in one another's embrace. In the darkness, the Sun is conceived once more, and at the winter solstice, the Great Lord of Light is birthed from the womb of she who is Mother and Matrix. This is the Goddess who claims the crown of the King of the Underworld and transforms it into the circle of rebirth as she places it around her neck, declaring, "Here is the circle of rebirth. Through you all pass out of life, but through me all may be born again."[40]

---

40 Starhawk, *The Spiral Dance*, 173.

THE DESCENDING ONES

Here I will provide a brief insight into several myths that encapsulate deities who descend. The descent, as always, is a poetic metaphor for the spiralling inward of the seeker into the dark forever-womb and the rebirth into light (enlightenment) as a whole being.

Freya: Norse Goddess of Earth, Fertility, Love, Magick, Sexuality, and War

In her own hall in Asgard, the heavenly realm of the gods, Freya was gripped one morning by a sudden urge to pass by the rainbow—the pathway that bridged the worlds—and descend into Midgard. The golden goddess was unsure of the origin of this motivation, but the instinctual propulsion was too strong to ignore. Once in Midgard, the goddess entered a cave, and as she did so, she began to weep her tears of amber and gold. Deeper and deeper she travelled, as the narrow path wound to and fro, until Freya came upon a shining forge, in which the Brisings, the four dwarves of the four directions, bore a radiant, golden necklace—the Brisingamen.

As her piercing sight beheld the glowing necklet, the goddess felt such a great pang of lust and need for the Brisingamen that it almost broke her chest. She demanded at once that the necklace be hers in exchange for exorbitant amounts of gold and silver. However, the dwarves declined this offer and instead asked the lovely goddess if she would lie with them all, one night each. Freya agreed to the proposal, and so for four nights she lay with each of the dwarves in turn, and on the fifth morning she claimed her quarry: the Brisingamen. The golden goddess ascended adorned in the necklace of Brisings and returned to her hall in Asgard.

All the while, Loki, the trickster god, had been quietly observing the events as they unfolded. In his constant desire for chaos, he decided to visit the all-father—the one-eyed, terrible, war-waging Odin—and inform him of Freya's newly acquired treasure. At once,

Odin was beset with rage and demanded that Loki steal the Brisings' necklace from the goddess Freya as she slept. Loki agreed to the foul assignment and transformed into a fly in order to penetrate the fortitude of Freya's hall. He then had to transform once more into a flea in order to be small enough that he could move unnoticed on the goddess's skin and ultimately sting her so that she would turn in her sleep and expose the clasp of the necklace to him. Loki undid the Brisingamen and stole away into the night with the treasure.

Freya awoke in the morning only to find that her beloved necklace had been stolen. She knew immediately that it was the work of Loki and that it had been sanctioned by Odin. Trembling with almighty and righteous anger, the goddess charged into the hall of Odin and ordered Odin to return the Brisingamen. Odin refused; however, if Freya would set the kings of Midgard against each other in bloody battle, the terrible god would consider returning the stolen necklace. Freya pondered over this predicament, but before she agreed to the new bargain, the goddess required that of the fallen in battle, she be allowed to gather and collect souls for her own glory in the heavens. The two agreed on this pact, and thus Freya became not only a goddess of fertility, magick, sexuality, and love, but also of war.

Inanna: Sumerian Goddess of Fertility, Love, Magick, and War

Inanna, the great queen of the above, of the star-glistening heavens, cast her mind to the great below, and thus she took up the sacred measures of the goddess—the crown, the wig, the lapis lazuli necklace, the egg-shaped beads, the dress, the holy mascara, and the pectoral. With Ninshubur—the vizier of her temple—in tow, Inanna began the journey to the underworld.

As the two travelled, Inanna instructed Ninshubur to go to the Great Ones once she arrived and passed into the shadow-realm of her sister, the dark queen Erishkigal. Firstly, Ninshubur was to return to Inanna's various temples and begin the long lament. The vizier was also to visit Enlil, god of the atmosphere, and plead with him that

Inanna would not be subjugated in the underworld. If Enlil would not agree to aid Inanna, then Ninshubur was to go to Nanna, the god of the moon, and appeal to him. If Nanna would not help, then Ninshubur was to visit Enki, the god of the sweet waters, and it would be there, in the temple of the wise lord Enki, that Ninshubur would be welcomed, and the goddess would be ensured divine witness. For Enki knew of the secrets of the heavenly waters—that they will fall to bring forth the green shoots from the bowels of the underworld. Inanna would bring life once more to the world. She would bring the harvest!

The two finally arrived at the gates of the underworld. Ninshubur left immediately to carry out the mission given to her by Inanna. The great goddess yelled to the guard and demanded passage to see her sister Erishkigal. The guard rushed first to report Inanna's presence and desires to his dark queen. Erishkigal laughed and instructed her guard to bolt each of the seven gates of the underworld, but to allow her sister entry.

The guard, Neti, brought Inanna in through the doors of the underworld and then to the first gate. Here he removed her headdress. Inanna, distressed by this infringement on her divine authority, questioned Neti as to his assault. Neti merely rebuked the goddess and instructed her to keep and honour the customs of the underworld in silence. At each gate one of the seven *me* (divine measures) was stripped from Inanna, until, bare-naked, the goddess was presented to Erishkigal in her royal chambers. The dark goddess called forth to the Anunnaki, the seven judges of the realm, and in anger and resentment the judgment was passed that Inanna be turned into a corpse and be hanged from a hook.

For three days and three nights Inanna hung lifeless. In the world of the living, Ninshubur had begun the great lament and had visited the three deities. Enki understood his task in securing the goddess's return to the earth while keeping and honouring the law and custom of the underworld.

Erishkigal called for her guard Neti and demanded that he call forth the attendance of the gods and goddesses and sprinkle Inanna's corpse with life-giving water—the gift of Enki. Enlivened once more, the goddess was given her freedom. As she passed back through the seven gates of the underworld, each of the sacred measures were returned. Inanna ascended into the bright world above; however, in exchange for this gift to the people of the land, the harvest lord Tammuz was to be given to the underworld, into the dark queen's keeping.

Persephone: Greek Goddess of Initiation, Spring, and the Underworld

Persephone, daughter of Demeter and Zeus, was gathering flowers with the daughters of Okeanos in the fields when a hundred-blossomed narcissus caught her undivided attention. She plucked the flower from the earth, and at the exact moment she did, the earth opened and the dark lord Hades rose up from the underworld in his horse-driven chariot. He scooped up the young goddess and retreated back into the shadow realms.

The goddess of grain and growth, Demeter, heard the cries of her daughter but was too late to save Persephone, as she arrived at the scene with nothing but a plucked narcissus. The wise and ancient titan Hekate came to console the goddess and suggested that the two visit Helios in the heavens, whose great eye sees all. Upon visiting Helios, the solar titan attempted to soothe the distressed mother as he relayed the events as they had unfolded—Zeus and Hades had arranged for Persephone to be married to Hades as his bride, and thus she was to become the queen of the dead. Furious, Demeter began a long lament for her daughter. She walked the earth in misery and torment, bearing before her the bright firebrand of Hekate, always in eternal vigilance and hope that her sweet-lipped daughter might return.

In her righteous anger at the gods of Olympos for their unforgivable deed, Demeter withdrew her power and vitality from the earth, and the first winter arrived. The crops failed, and there was no harvest to be had for the people of the earth, so they in turn withdrew supplication to the gods. The gods of Olympos were unused to the distress and discontent of their worshippers, and inwardly many of the deities were concerned whether the lack of sacrifices would deplete their own immortal power. The gods pleaded with Zeus to send Hermes to the underworld to bargain with Hades and to have Persephone returned to the bright world above—and to Demeter.

Hermes, in his role as psychopomp (deliverer of souls), was one of the few beings who could traverse the worlds, and thus he gained entry into Hades' realm. There he spoke in haste with Hades, who agreed it was proper that Persephone be returned to Demeter and the world above. However, before Persephone ascended, Hades gave her six pomegranate seeds, representing the six months of the year in which the waning forces would reign on the earth. He spoke his eternal love to the trim-ankled goddess, and because she had been witness to the mercy and kindness of this ill-regarded god, she knew in her heart that the flame of love had been kindled, and she could not leave Hades forever. She ate the seeds in knowledge that she would see her husband once more and that she would forever be a queen.

The goddess ascended, and so the daughter and the mother embraced, and life returned in a flourish to the lands. The spring returned and with it the warmth, light, and vitality that is abundance, fertility, and growth. Persephone was now both the goddess of the springtide as well as the awesome queen of the dead. She had become more than she had ever dreamed, and she was happy.

The Ritual of Descent:
Becoming the Circle of Rebirth

This ritual is designed as an initiatory rite that aims to facilitate the journey of the descent into the underworld. It is a highly transformative rite that should not be undertaken lightly. As with anything, I write rituals for the greater Pagan community in awareness of the multiplicity of traditions and ceremonial inclinations, so please observe each step, or instruction, as a guideline only, and feel free to embellish, delete, and change completely at will.

I will draw upon the mythos of the Crescent-Crowned Goddess to whom the WildWood Tradition gives honour; however, please use a mythos or story from a culture or deity which you are greatly inspired by or devoted to (see above for a few myths/ stories relating to those who descend). This ritual blends British Traditional Witchcraft, Stregheria, and WildWood as its basis for inspiration, theme, and direction. You will also notice that this ritual does not follow the land, sky, and sea model I have developed for the affirming/celebratory ritual for each realm at the end of each part of this book. However, the three realms are definitely present in the informing cosmology of this ritual of descent. This ritual was also inspired by a WildWood priestess, Ratna Devi, who wove the banishing/empowerment exercise through the elements into a new moon ritual she designed for our inner court. It is to my beloved inner court of the Coven of the WildWood—Awen, Arione, Helona, Ratna Devi, Rowan, Luna, Meriel, Serica, and Saule—that I dedicate this ritual, and to our lady of the moon, the Crescent-Crowned Goddess.

For this ritual, human aid is very welcome; it is up to you to decide whether you feel best conducting the ritual in complete solitude or with the help of a close Pagan friend.[41] Also, for a ritual of this magnitude (in terms of the facilitation of an initiatory experience), it is a wise idea to fast for the entire day leading to the ritual, which should begin as the sun starts to set. Wake just after sunrise and begin the fast.[42]

You will need:

- Censer (charcoal disc with a mixed incense of cypress, frankincense, myrrh, and wormwood)—to be placed in the air quadrant
- White taper candle—to be placed in the fire quadrant
- Chalice (filled with spring/rain/sea water)—to be placed in the water quadrant
- Pentacle/flowers—to be placed in the earth quadrant
- Crown/ivy wreath—to be placed in the centre for spirit
- Staff/sword—to be placed in the centre for spirit
- Black translucent veil (some sight is needed)
- Clairvoyant-clarifying eyewash (see page 92)
- One single flower (appropriate to both you and the deity)
- Hand-held mirror

Prepare and lay out the ritual space before the ritual begins. Just as indicated above, place each tool in the appropriate quadrant (or centre) of the circle, ensuring there is enough space for you to comfortably reside within; a diameter of 4–5 metres should work well. From here on, I will be describing the ritual directions as if another Pagan or magickal friend is assisting you in your ceremony. If you are conducting the ritual in solitude, simply adjust the directions to suit your circumstance.

---

41 I say Pagan friend because a knowledge of the theory and practice of Pagan ritual is necessary for the dynamic flow of the initiatory experience.

42 For a good grounding on the technicalities and spirituality of fasting, please see Raven Digitalis's *Shadow Magick Compendium* (Llewellyn, 2008).

As the sun begins to set, stand at the eastern point of the circle (outside) and face the west. Ground and centre as you watch the sun dip beneath the horizon, and at the moment the last rays of the day disappear, have your friend silently drape the black veil over your head so that your face is covered and vision obscured. Stand at the boundary of the eastern point of the circle, open your arms in the traditional (Wiccan) Goddess/ Isis pose, and say:

> *I surrender to the all-encompassing darkness. I begin the descent. I call upon the blessed Lady of Moon and Magick to guide me on this path into the underworld. May the silver-led sea bless me as I journey into shadow.*

Kneel and bow your head as you cross your arms in the traditional (Wiccan) God pose, and say:

> *I surrender to the gate of death. I am descending. I call upon the dread Lord of Death and Decay to receive me into the underworld. May the broad land bless me as I journey into shadow.*

By this time, darkness should have fallen, and there is no light. Remain kneeling while your friend casts the circle and forms the space in whichever way suits your tastes and inclinations. The elements should be formally addressed here, too. As this is happening, keep silent and open to the experience that is to be found at the heart of the circle of rebirth. If you like, have your friend chant these words while casting the circle (to affirm and clarify the intent and purpose of the whole ritual):

Circle of rebirth, I conjure thee
By all that is, so blessed be
To be a space between the worlds
To bring forth spirit to unfurl.

A door, or gateway, must now be cut at the northeastern point of the circle, and you are to be admitted—once again in complete and resounding silence. Your friend may now either leave the area entirely or remain quietly outside of the circle as an observer of the rite as it unfolds. However, ensure that your assistant will be close by, as they will need to be present to help complete and seal the ritual. For now, you will be alone within the circle to meet with the dark and to be transformed and reborn.

Kneel in the centre of the circle facing the west, and once again call forth to the king of the dead:

> *Lord of the underworld, you are the consoler of our beloved*
> *dead who have passed and who by your grace find rest in your*
> *realms. In earnest and deep conviction, I call upon you. I call*
> *you as witness and guardian of my descent. I call unto you,*
> *for you made the first Witch, and I am a son/daughter of the*
> *spirit of the Witch. In my descent, I seek initiation once more.*
> *I seek rebirth into the ways of old and into deeper knowledge*
> *and understanding of self, and through reflection of self,*
> *wisdom of the great mystery that is the cosmos. Blessed be.*

Turn to the east and kneel before the censer. Focus on a quality or trait you associate with air that you find binds you from liberation of self. Through the agent of air, let go of this quality, and in return cense yourself with the fragrant smoke as you invite in all benevolence and blessings of the spirit of air. In a deosil manner, repeat the same process with each element until you reach the centre—spirit.

To represent spirit in the centre are the crown/wreath and the staff/sword. The staff/sword should be laid down flat, with the hilt at the east and the tip of the blade at the west, running through the centre of the crown/wreath (also laid flat), which should be sitting in the centre of the circle.

Sit or kneel before these symbols of spirit and employ one of the trance techniques given in this book (or one of your own) to enter into an altered state of consciousness, which will help propel you into the realm of Death. Come fully face to face with the lord of the underworld himself, and by the rapture of his presence become entirely enfolded into his infinity. Understand the eternity of cycles and that there is always rebirth. It is said that at the climax of the Greater Eleusinian Mysteries[43] in ancient Greece, the hierophant held up an ear of corn/grain and all gathered beheld the mysteries of life and death in one succinct moment of divine revelation. This too was the symbol Persephone showed to me as a farewell after I had physically visited the ancient temple grounds of Eleusis in modern-day Greece.

In the cold embrace of Death, allow yourself to die; to break apart; to dissolve into nothingness. Let the fear melt away, and become at peace with the fate that will befall us all. Let the scythe of the pale dark lord reap you, but keep eternal faith in the reality and divine truth of rebirth. Be safe in the knowledge that nothing ever truly dies; it can only transform. These truths are even enshrined in the halls of fundamental science: Newton stated that energy cannot be created or destroyed, it can only change form. We are all energy.

---

43 The Eleusinian Mysteries were the ancient Greek ceremonial celebrations that centred around the mythos of Demeter the grain mother and her rising and descending daughter Persephone, queen of the underworld and lady of spring. The mysteries were broken into "lesser" and "greater," the former being celebrated in the spring and the latter in the autumn.

In whichever way the initiation comes, receive it. This is your time to be. Take in the moment of eternity, and let it destroy, scatter, conjure, soothe, heal, and rebirth you. When you feel that the intensity of the experience is receding, stand, and let the veil fall. Face up towards the heavens and stretch your arms and hands upward as if to praise the All-Eternal, the Divine, and say:

I am all that there is, all that there was, and all that ever will be. By the blessings and peace of our lord of death and decay, and by the luminous guiding truth of our lady of moon and magick, am I born anew as their holy child. I am balanced by the four elements of life, and thus I have been charged by the fifth—the spirit. May the angel-lit campfires of the sky light my way and inspire me as I journey forever into eternity. Blessed be!

Using the clairvoyant-clarifying eyewash, acknowledge your divine birthright to see clearly always. Place the crown/wreath upon your head, and take up the staff/sword and affirm to yourself that you are divine and wholly within your rights to exist and to do so in happiness, peace, and wisdom.

Farewell the deities and the elements, and unravel the circle as is your way. Clap your hands together loudly three times to signal for your friend to return (make sure your friend is aware of the claps as a signal to return prior to the ritual). Your assistant will return to you with a flower in hand as a gift and a token of your rebirth into life. They will also hold a mirror facing towards you so that you are able to see, in clarity, your face and the soul that dwells beyond the eyes that see. Receive the flower with deep gratitude and keep it in water on your altar as a memory of your own descent.

Blessed be.

INITIATION

If I were to come forth from the womb and speak clearly the words of wisdom and truth, would I be believed? If I were to rise with the sun at the dawn of the new day and whisper the secrets of the worlds, would I be heeded? If I were to raise the storms and bind you to my will, would I be stronger for it? If I were to promise you the glory of these gifts, would I be respected as a mighty being?

If an initiate desires any of the above, then it is quite apparent that they have only superficially crossed the threshold into the mysteries— or, rather, not done so at all. A true initiate[44] is interested only in walking the path of the initiate—the never-ending journey of conscious service to the All-Self, which manifests in myriad expressions of life. Of course, the vastness (and the honest simplicity) of the implications of such a life cannot be surmised on paper or through verbal conversation alone. As those of the mysteries are apt to say, "The mysteries can only be experienced."

Initiation means, quite simply, "to begin." To initiate is to establish something new with blazing purpose and clear intent. To be initiated is to be born again—to have one's eyes opened to greater understanding and intimacy with the "thatness that is." In my tradition, a dedicant (a member of the inner court) can formally begin priest/ess training (towards their initiation) after six months of dedication. Priest/ess training generally takes six months of weekly intensives, though it never truly stops. When the priesthood (myself included) discuss the meaning of "initiation" and what it is to be initiated with Witches in priest/ess training, we make sure that it is plainly and beautifully communicated that initiation is forever; we "begin" again and again eternally. Learning never stops, and thus initiation is a forever journey.

---

44 One who has consciously and fruitfully become keenly aware of the holy communion that is kinship and oneness with the Divine that is. As my friend and fellow WildWood priest Awen would say, "An initiate is a witness to wonder."

The amount of times I have felt truly initiated are numerous, and not all of them happened within a ritual/circle context.

A Witch understands life and the experiences that go hand in hand with that mystery to be one great circle that we cast (reaffirm) again in every moment. The importance of ceremonial initiation in the context of mystery traditions such as Witchcraft is that the ritual helps to facilitate an unbinding and an opening up to the freedom that is our gods-given birthright! Often, while having my personal devotional ritual every week, I will reaffirm this sacred truth for myself by reciting my own personalisation of a traditional Craft verse: "I come to the charge neither bound nor free, but it is here, within the circle that is in all places, that I find my freedom."

For me, the Craft has always concerned freedom—the freedom to accept that I am a powerful being in my own right, and therefore I am able to live my life and channel the currents of change and evolution to aid my journeying through the woven web of Wyrd. I am a Witch and a priest, and I have focussed on the equilibrium—and, indeed, the implicit complementation—between these two states of being. In my mind and heart, the Witch is aware, and the priest harnesses this awareness, enhances it, and channels it towards service and devotion to the gods, the tribe/community (including the environment/earth which sustains us), and self. However, this is not to say that a Witch who does not consider herself a priestess is not on a path of service or devotion. Indeed, in my opinion, being a Witch, at least in the modern revived traditions, implies priesthood.

When one is initiated as a Witch and priest/ess (as the Wiccan rites testify), one is opened to the vital current that is born of the great mystery and returns to it. If we are initiated into that current, we become vessels for and of the great mystery, and that is a journey one never forgets.

One can never fully describe initiation or the phenomenon of this particular magickal rite of passage, as words do no justice to the truth and core of the experience. However, here I have assembled a few beautiful words and expressions from a variety of Pagan friends who have been, are, and will continue to be initiated.

Initiation means to become a witness to wonder, to the great wonder of the mystery...to become the great wisdom.
—Awen, initiated priest of the WildWood
Tradition (Coven of the WildWood)

Initiation...it's as if delicate threads of the most dense yet light metal have woven their way into my spinal cord, my bones, my veins. It reminds me. It holds me to what is sacred, to the very centre of what I am. It is with me in moments of terror and joy, and it is simply me, myself...which will always be, to me, the greatest mystery of all.
—Arione, initiated priestess of the WildWood
Tradition (Coven of the WildWood)

I entered with hands bound, blindfolded, and relying on being led to show my perfect trust. After the physical release, I was presented with a coven robe, which I changed into within the circle. These physical forms symbolised internal changes of clear sight, free movement, and a new presentation of myself to the world. To me, initiation was a ceremonial ritual, a recognition and a reward for hard work and a transformation into the full freedom of equality and community within the coven. The ceremony was as powerful as a shooting star in the night sky, full of joy and spirit but also serious and sober.
—SpirAl, initiated Witch of Earthwyrm Coven

My initiation into Paganism opened a totally new way of life for me—a realization that I was looking at everything from a different perspective and deriving more from each day because of it. It's been many years since that change took place for me, and the differences are still apparent and continuing each moment. From that time onwards, life has taken on a glow that grows ever stronger and more purposeful.
—Marye-Ann Azzarello, initiated Witch
of Earthwyrm Coven and Coven of the Two Sisters

*For me, initiation marked the beginning of my commitment to the
Pagan way. I had learned enough by then to know that this was
the path for me, and also enough to know that there was still a
lifetime of learning in front of me. I think initiation is a way of
saying, "My feet are on the path; now let's see where it leads."*

—Morganna, initiated Witch and
high priestess of Earthwyrm Coven

*Initiation.
Know it, name it, step forward and claim it!
Here is the mantle of priestess—take it.
A long journey lies behind you,
So let me remind you,
Of the long nights of doubt,
Of the days of fun and dancing,
Of the way your mind cleared after learning
That you do not have to be perfect,
Only willing to offer your service.
Yes, when you made your first attempt,
You didn't know that you could take this step;
So celebrate as we offer acknowledgement,
Be bold although we can't hold your hand
To help you over this threshold.
Today you need to stand alone before the gods
Knowing it, naming it,
Finally claiming it;
That you have a desire for service
That you are their priestess.*

—Helona Moverin, initiated priestess
of the WildWood Tradition (Coven of the WildWood)

*Initiation is the acceptance within yourself of your connection with
the greater worlds around you. It is taking the next step on your path
and walking with strength, knowledge, and courage in your heart.*

—Shiray, urban shaman

Initiation is not a stroll in the park. Initiation is a journey through the hidden and shadowed crevice to what lies beyond. However, the initiate is not truly alone: their coveners, the Mighty Ones and the Goddess and God all witness and partake in the journey.
—Dyffeg, second-degree priestess
and Witch, Circle Coven

Initiation means to offer one's self to the gods, to experience not just their presence but their acceptance. It is a journey of humility and sacrifice of ego.
—Sarah, initiated priestess, Circle Coven

Initiation is the affirmation of my oneness with the earth and all of her inhabitants—human and non-human, spiritual and physical, animate and inanimate—in the ever-increasing web of life that connects us all through time and space.
—Linda, initiated priestess of a
Celtic Pagan path (solitary)

Initiation is the end of a journey with the gods and the elements and is the beginning of a new one.
—Amaris, initiated priestess, Circle Coven

Initiation means to begin a journey towards self-discovery and self-mastery. Quite simply, it is to initiate the process of unravelling who and what we truly are. It is the turning point of an individual's life, where one has decided once and for all to know oneself. Initiation only happens once, and the process of unfolding is ongoing. You cannot turn back or unlearn what you have learnt. Once you have begun, you cannot go back.
—Dennis, initiated priest of Janicot

Initiation is the clarity of knowing so greatly and feeling so deeply the mysteries, and then realising all over again you know nothing!
—Saule, initiate of a Celtic Wiccan tradition
and the WildWood Tradition

The Lord of Death, he came to me,
As I beheld the grail
Of wonder, joy, enlightenment,
And thus begins my tale.
In golden light and hues divine,
I knelt before the king;
He handed me the axe of death
I trembled in his ring.
Blunt blade, long staff,
A sceptre proud, of tearing life from life;
Of blood, of loss, of pain, of grief
And causing all but strife.
But then the Mother came to me
And whispered secrets old;
Beside the gruesome blade
She placed a glory to behold.
Beside the blood-stained blade
She placed a sickle moon,
She sang to me of rebirth
From the darkness of her womb.
The Goddess smiled and knelt and said,
"I love you, you are mine."
I knelt and kissed her silver lips
And witnessed the Divine.
For within each seed therein lies
A story to unfold;
And it is life and it is death
A glory to behold.

—Eilan, initiated priest of the WildWood Tradition
and of the goddess Persephone and the lady Aphrodite

THE GIFT
OF PERSEPHONE

Her flawless, shadow-riddled face stared soullessly back from the ancient mirror, eyes unblinking and lips poised to reveal the white caps of two perfect rows of teeth. The glass was smudged, and the concave depths seemed to lap a pool of eternity. Eurydike lay on her side, her unbridled pink flesh resting against the soft fabric of perfectly pressed linen sheets and satin pillows. Her left arm propped itself up to frame her elegant elfin chin while she ceaselessly traced patterns with her tapered fingers. Her raven-black hair shone eerily beneath the subtle glow of the crescent moon as its lunar liquid slid down the arch of her delicate back, forming an intricacy of rivers and streams against the fine lines that composed her young skin. Eurydike glanced up to see a snow-white owl perched upon the windowsill, an ocean of black crashing formidably against its stark luminosity.

The owl tilted its head as if to study the porcelain figure. Secrets and stories spilled forth from the inky midnight tones of the bird's endlessly open eyes and began to dance evocatively with the undulating shadows.

Eurydike watched as the owl performed its task and then took flight, the surrounding darkness absorbing it completely as if it were a taint or the owl a shapeshifter. Though the owl had passed into the shadowy passage that was the gaping yawn of night, Eurydike felt its presence linger on, an imprint set into the fibres of air that clung like weather-beaten strips of fabric to a rain-soaked body. Stifling her own delicate yawn, Eurydike inwardly affirmed her decision. She had not taken the road to the west for many a year; however, the memories of the journey had never left her, and in the deepest moments, when solitude was the cloak, they swarmed through her mind. Driven by an insatiable lust to reunite with the forward consciousness that was the present-being, Eurydike embarked on a pilgrimage along the road to what can only be known by unknowing oneself.

Drawn to and empowered by the heartwoven stretch of mystery that was the gods and their livelihood, Eurydike rose reverently from her bed, taking care not to crease the sheets. A mist gathered at her feet and began to spiral, surrounding her slight frame as if fueled by some serpentine divinity. Eurydike heard the soft hiss and smelt the cypress and juniper of the chthonic temple as if its scent had remained eternally imprinted upon the soft palate of her tongue. A lilt began to slide self-consciously through her lips, escaping before any inhibition was able to bar its way. The lilt became a lull and the lull became a chant and the chant a song, until the golden muses themselves forsook all their endeavours just to listen. The cosmos, the ribboning current of life, was filled to its outermost with the vibrating presence of the spell and echoed back the story of creation itself. For Eurydike's song was made of the essence of magick, and while she was no great Witch like the famed Medea, she knew the path to the underworld was won by such a spell as was unravelling. Then, as if a lock had been slid out of place, there was a series of hastened clicks, and a pure vision unfolded before Eurydike's eyes.

First there was a river, channelled through small openings within the earth, flanked by settled stone and veins of treasure. The river, black as pitch, emerged from the dragon's carved path into a field of soft yellow light that came as honey runs spilt. There were many happy souls, and they feasted and drank from a spring that wove further back, until no trace of its source could be marked. Eurydike then noticed a dark man who seemed the patron of the realm, crowned and with woven bands of crop and blossom about his arms as if the gathering had bedecked him with these gifts in honour of his kindness and generosity to them. He was a king, and feeding around his feet was a black cockerel, sparsely snowed upon, though the light shone from its preened feather coat in a golden hue that seemed to say, "Here is one blessed." Then the light began to dim, and the field of laughter and light faded as the coarse and violent journey through the howling halls of Tartaros began.

Pain and suffering was the brand endured by the damned and forgotten, whose destiny it was to linger trapped and tortured forevermore. There was unearthly shrieking and a keening undertone that clipped finely at Eurydike's heart. There were stretches of blood-stained platters on which the beating hearts of the damned were as potatoes to blunt knives. Tartaros was a hollow veil and not truly a place of substance, existing mercilessly on the periphery of Hades.

My daughter, came a voice. Eurydike sat within a royal chamber, splendid in its subtlety and Spartan grace. While there were few things to fill the grandeur of the room, each one was a miraculous beauty. The throne that Eurydike had awakened to seemed at first the work of the wood-realms; however, upon second glance, she noticed the soft gleam of obsidian and the flash of rainbow that signalled its profound depths. Upon the throne, however, was a woman—a woman who wore a soft, trailing white gown that neither hung loosely nor hugged her form. Her long hair was black and shone from the rich oils and spices that had been lathered into the fibres. Her eyes were waterlike jewels embedded in a porcelain face of serene expression. Her blood-red lips were enhanced by the glistening juices of the pomegranate, and her supple breasts were nursed by a modest neckline. All was still. An all-pervasive silence wove its way into the core of Eurydike's being until she found herself kneeling, head bowed to the woman before her. Suddenly all Eurydike had ever known had been washed away in a torrent of massing shadows, writhing like Medusa's own crown. Eurydike knew then that the woman before her was more than and exactly as she appeared. She was the Lady of Paradox, the Veil and the Veiled, the Key to the Mystery, the Queen of Hades, and—of course—she who bears the promise of spring, the Kore...Persephone.

She sung the spell, and the cosmos began to quake—all came undone in that moment underlying time.

Persephone spoke:

I am the grey of the storm on the horizon—the moment before lightning cleaves the shaking air. I am the wild mistress of shadows forming, swimming, and ceaselessly morphing one to the next. I am the serpent-mother who coils in each shadow as scale and bows in deepest gratitude to the silver-blessed sea. I am she who has risen and she who has descended the labyrinthine-way to meet with and court the prince of death, whose name is aflame upon the crest of my heart. I am the key and I am the mystery, and I am forever written in the Book of Truth as she whose sword of light shall bring illumination to the troubled mind and peace to those whose hearts are yoked to fear's oppression. I am freedom! I am the Kore! I am unashamed in wisdom! I am beauteous and terrible! I am in awe and overflowing—and yet with stony silence, I am the exacter of justice at the end of days. Come unto me and let the secret spill forth from my blood-stained lips—thou art free! I shall give thee return to the bright world above when the heart despairs in forgotten prayer, for I am she who knows Lethe and memory, and intoxicates one with the other. I am illusion, and I am truth. I am priestess of the way in between, and I am the lover of being. I am Hagnes, the holy one, and the Megala Thea, the great one. I am Soteira, the saviour, and Daeira, the knowing one. Abide within me, and I shall whisper the All into the shimmering silence that you may drink deep from the abyss. I am Persephone.

RITUAL

This ritual can be celebrated either as a solitary or with a group. It is a Neopagan ritual with Celtic, Wiccan, and Witchcraft influences.

You will need:

- One white taper candle
- Incense made up of 3 drops rosemary essential oil, 1 part rose petals, 2 parts Celtic sea salt
- Brazier and charcoal disc
- White cotton veil
- Low seat or cushion
- One large chalice (filled with spring water or rain water)

The sea ritual will work best if it is carried out beneath a tree. You can choose to set up an altar, but in this case, simplicity is key.

Ground and Centre

Ground and centre using the tree of life alignment meditation. Now, in this calm and centred state, verbally acknowledge the indigenous guardians and spirits of the place, and ask for their blessings on the ritual. Now it is time to form the space (to cast the circle).

Cast the Circle

The circle will be cast by passing a chalice of blessed water around the circle from person to person, each drinking and beginning and ending in the east. As the chalice is passed and each person sips from it, the following is said:

> *As I drink from the womb of the Mother,*
> *so do I take in the essence of the circle of rebirth.*
> *May my lips speak this circle into being.*

If you are conducting the rite in solitude, walk deosil, pouring the water from the chalice in a circle until one full circumambulation has been made, and then drink from the chalice deeply. Complete the casting by reciting the words above.

At the right time, the circle should be affirmed:

> *The circle is cast. I / We are now between the*
> *worlds, in all the worlds. So mote it be.*

Acknowledge Land, Sky & Sea

If alone, make all three gestures independently while mentally or verbally acknowledging the corresponding realm. In a group situation, appoint three different people to a respective realm (one for land, one for sky, and one for sea). The gestures and words for each realm are as follows:

Land: Place both hands on the ground—*"By the land…"*

Sky: Hold hands open and up to the sky—*"By the sky…"*

Sea: Cup both hands together in front of the navel—*"And by the sea…"*

All together, say, *"By the ancient trinity, so mote it be!"*

To seal the blessing, trace a triquetra (⟨triquetra symbol⟩) in the air with the first two fingers of your power/dominant hand.

The candle (which is placed at the foot of the tree) is lit to represent the fire of the Divine, where the three realms are one.

Blessing of the Sea

Now is the time to pour personal libations of water under the tree. As you do this, understand that you are nourishing the mighty roots of the world tree that sustains us all.

If you are celebrating this ritual with a group, you may stand (or appoint someone else) as challenger, and recite the following charge to inspire everyone before the libations are poured:

My sisters and brothers in the sea, I bless you in the name of the ancient Mother's womb, which brings us into dreaming and sustains us to our core. We are each a wave upon the ocean, yearning to reach the shore once more. The salty sea yearns always to fulfil its charge of love to all. The lands are divided and united by the seas of our ancestors. In honour of their memory, the wisdom of their hearts, and the power of the placid calm of the sea and the mighty terror of the ocean, do we pour these libations in offering.

Guided Sea Meditation

A boat, washed ashore on timeless waves made white by the soft glow of the full moon sailing in the sky. There, in the placid sea, in the ravaged ocean, in the terrifying, vast, and forever womb from whence we came, whisper secrets long forgotten. The salt-sea air sends this ancient wisdom into the beating hearts of all those who wonder and yearn: I am wonder...to be yearned for, to be known intimately in the centre, at the very edge and beyond...I am death, come unto me, she whispers.

The sea is for the journeyer who has travelled across the majesty of the broad earth. Its cool, pure embrace receives the dreamer whose eyes alight with the ember-glow of the stars as they blaze throughout the black sea that holds the lustre of the heavens. I am the sea, come unto me…in death's black, cold embrace, I give you rest and eternity…in the forever-time, the mysteries are made ever sweeter, she whispers.

Just as I am the ocean, which is the matrix of life, I am also the cauldron to which all return, and the journey across the sunless sea into the great beyond. I am feared and despised, just as I am dreamed of in love and adoration, and the Old Ones chant Mari, Maria, Mariana, Miriam, Mor, Morgana…these luminous names are many, and the blood that pulses in the veins of these blessed ones is the divine water that nourishes the soul and quenches the thirst of the wandering wonderer—the seeker, the fool. It is time; come unto me, she whispers.

I am the great divider between lands, but without me they are disparate and discrete; with me they are united and joined within the Mother, who is wholeness and connection. These gifts are the greatest magick the mystery can be. Look into my depths, my shallows, my effervescent sheen by lightfall, and know that, in seeking, we pierce the veil and grow instead to wear it. One who is initiated by the sea will inherit all that comes into being and all that leaves it as well…I am the Goddess, who can never be hidden; all is within my watery embrace.

Atop the highest mountain and cradled within the luscious, evergreen valleys, I am known and revered. The ocean is in all, and it runs through all. The rivers, the streams, the tributaries, and the bubbling brooks are my dancing daughters, my spiralling arms as I delve further and further into the presence that becomes life when it is given soil to seed. I am the mother of all life, and I pour my love out upon the earth. I am the sea…come unto me, I whisper.

Calling Upon the Oracle

If in a group situation, only one must be appointed to take on the mantle of oracle for the remainder of the ritual, though for practical and spiritual purposes the choice should be made prior to the beginning of the ritual, if not at least a few hours beforehand. If the ritual is to be conducted in solitude, consider bringing a tape recorder or pen and paper into the circle so that you may read/listen to the words later on, once you are grounded and in a receptive, calm state.[45]

The oracle is to don the white veil and enter or induce a light trance. The incense is to be waved back and forth in front of the oracle and all around the body. Once the oracle is settled into an altered state, questions may be put forward for the oracle to respond to while channeling the wisdom of the gods/universe/spirits/etc. This is not to be a drawing down or trance possession; rather, the oracle becomes a conduit for cosmic information to flow through for the benefit of spiritual reflection and tribal/communal understanding.

Once the session is over, the oracle is to slowly and gradually return to the former state of consciousness. Light food and drink is to be provided to aid in the oracle's grounding. Leave a few moments here for reflection.

Open the Space

Snuff out the candle flame and acknowledge the blessings of the three realms, the world tree that joins them, and the indigenous guardians and spirits of place. Open the circle by moving widdershins and visualising the sphere of light dispersing into the air and the earth. Do this in silence, as this can help to ground the excess energy that your body may retain after magickally intensive work. Eat and drink something to further ground the body.

---

45 The solitary can hold internal questions in the forefront of their mind as the channeling begins. The answers will then be recorded and played back later.

CONCLUSION

*The highest heavens can lead to the depths of the underworld,
and the center of the underworld can lead to the realm of
stars. As above, so below. Everything is connected.*
—Christopher Penczak, *The Temple of Shamanic Witchcraft*

In the course of writing this book, I underwent quite a few massive
changes in my life. My books *Spirited: Taking Paganism Beyond the Circle*
and *Crafting the Community* were published. I began a health degree in
Western herbal medicine at college. I entered the intimacy of a loving
relationship, and I forged plans to move to another city and to branch
a new coven of the WildWood Tradition. These examples are the
most overt surface changes that have occurred in this time, and yet my
inner landscape has transformed so drastically that on many levels, I
have come to embrace an entirely new identity. This is the way of the
Wild Witch—with change and transformation comes new life, and it
is only pure and good that we go with the flow and embrace it!

The concept for this guidebook on deepening Pagan magick and
spirituality through the Celtic ancient trinity arose amidst the striking
natural beauty of Ireland. I was blessed enough to spend two weeks
in September 2008 travelling the Emerald Isle with two amazing close

friends. I recall the exact place in which I was moved to journal in my Book of Shadows that I had officially decided my next writing project would be this book. I remember the raw passion and excitement, and I couldn't wait to return home to the familiarity and security of my own computer and begin to really create something practical and inspiring for those Pagans and magickal folk desiring deeper insights into our spirituality in this modern world. I entered into this project imbued with the bright fire of Celtic romanticism and have concluded, in my opinion, with a highly eclectic guidebook on how to develop shamanic skills to infuse one's Craft with blazing purpose and a keen desire to serve.

The Celtic culture and spirituality was one of refinement, but at the deepest core, the Celts held highest the virtue of *imbas* or *awen*—the fire in the head, the divine inspiration—the poetic life force that animates consciousness and calls it to thrive. It has been my endeavour throughout my life and my writing to be a vessel, a conduit, and a channel for this force, and to allow it clearer passage into this world so that it may manifest its beauty, wisdom, and truth for all to behold. I can only hope and pray that the *awen* will continue to flow through and touch as many people as it already does.

Modern Paganism is coming of age. We are finding our feet in this unsure world. Many of us are consciously working towards greater acceptance of our people and ways in broader society, and others, through their shining example, display to the world that "we are an old people, we are a new people, we are the same people, stronger than before." Nowadays, "Pagan" isn't such a dirty word, and it is rare that it causes offence. If we continue to claim with pride and zest the ancestral heritage that is buried deep within, then we continue to create a place at the table of the global citizens of the world. The wisdom that flows within the veins glows with the light of spirit.

For those of you who have discovered within these pages a format or context for delving deeper into Pagan spirituality, then please do not hesitate to take what you have learnt from here and create new and meaningful ways to interact with the forces/archetypes that stir within the mythos of what has inspired me to bring forth these words. Remember that to stand on the land, surrounded by the sea (which is also within), and to have the sky watching down on you is to be both between the realms and whole within them. The world tree, the great centre of the world, is in all places, at all times, and wherever you wander, you are there—this is the centre, you only have to awaken to the reality.

If, when you kneel under the world tree and look up through the spiralling branches, you feel a merging of oneness with the tree, then relax, surrender, and go with it. Everything is okay, all is well, and the gods are with you.

Sláinte, my friends! Journey well!

May the land ever open new vistas before you; may the sky always keep your ideals pure; and may the sea gift you the power of dreams. By the land, by the sky, and by the sea—by the ancient trinity, blessed be.

Gede Parma

BIBLIOGRAPHY

Aswynn, F. *Northern Mysteries & Magick*. USA: Llewellyn, 1998.

Bates, B. *The Way of Wyrd*. USA: Hay House, 2005.

Beth, R. *Lamp of the Goddess*. USA: Weiser, 1995.

Coughlin, J. J. *Ethics and the Craft*. USA: Waning Moon Publications, 2009.

Crosley, R. *The Vodou Quantum Leap*. USA: Llewellyn, 2000.

Crossley-Holland, K. *The Norse Myths*. USA: Pantheon Books, 1980.

Crowley, V. *Phoenix from the Flame*. UK: Thorsons, 1994.

Cunningham, S. *Cunningham's Encyclopedia of Magical Herbs*. USA: Llewellyn, 2000.

De Angeles, L. *Witchcraft: Theory and Practice*. USA: Llewellyn, 2000.

Denning, M., and O. Phillips. *Mysteria Magica*. USA: Llewellyn, 2004.

Diamant, A. *The Red Tent*. Australia: Allen and Unwin, 1998.

Digitalis, R. *Shadow Magick Compendium*. USA: Llewellyn, 2008.

Dunn, P. *Postmodern Magic*. USA: Llewellyn, 2005.

Farrar, J., and G. Bone. *Progressive Witchcraft*. USA: New Page Books, 2004.

Galenorn, Y. *Crafting the Body Divine: Ritual, Movement, and Body Art*. USA: Crossing Press, 2001.

Gerber, R. *Vibrational Medicine: The #1 Handbook of Subtle-Energy Therapies*. USA: Bear & Co., 2001.

Gimbutas, M. *The Goddesses and Gods of Old Europe* (second edition). USA: University of California Press, 2007.

———. *The Language of the Goddess*. USA: Harper San Francisco, 1995.

Grimassi, R. *Hereditary Witchcraft*. USA: Llewellyn, 1999.

———. *Witchcraft: A Mystery Tradition*. USA: Llewellyn, 2004.

———. *The Witches' Craft: The Roots of Witchcraft & Magical Transformation*. USA: Llewellyn, 2002.

Harrow, J. *Devoted To You*. USA: Citadel, 2003.

Heaven, R. *The Sin Eater's Last Confessions*. USA: Llewellyn, 2008.

Herbert, M. *Healing Quest*. USA: Samuel Weiser, 1997.

Johnson, K. *Witchcraft and the Shamanic Journey*. USA: Llewellyn, 1999.

Keeney, B. *Shaking Out the Spirits*. USA: Station Hill Press, 1994.

Krasskova, G. *Exploring the Northern Tradition*. USA: New Page Books, 2005.

McCoy, E. *Advanced Witchcraft*. USA: Llewellyn, 2004.

Parma, G. (editor) *Crafting the Community*. Australia: Conjunction Press, 2009.

Parma, G. *Spirited: Taking Paganism Beyond the Circle*. USA: Llewellyn, 2009.

Penczak, C. *The Temple of Shamanic Witchcraft*. USA: Llewellyn, 2005.

Pollack, R. *The Body of the Goddess*. UK: Vega, 2003.

Polson, W. *The Veil's Edge: Exploring the Boundaries of Magic*. USA: Citadel Press, 2003.

Roads, M. J. *Journey into Nature: A Spiritual Adventure*. USA: H. J. Kramer, 1990.

Starhawk. *The Spiral Dance* (10th anniversary edition). USA: Harper & Row, 1989.

———. *The Fifth Sacred Thing*. USA: Bantam, 1993.

———. *Dreaming the Dark* (15th anniversary edition). USA: Beacon Press, 1997.

Stein, C. *Persephone Unveiled: Seeing the Goddess and Freeing Your Soul*. USA: North Atlantic Books, 2006.

INDEX

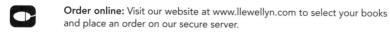

GEDE PARMA

SPIRITED

TAKING PAGANISM
BEYOND THE CIRCLE

"An exciting voice from a step beyond generation hex ... An excellent
guide not only for those in that generation, but for those of us seeking
to understand and deepen our relationship with them."
—CHRISTOPHER PENCZAK, author of *The Temple of High Witchcraft*

SPIRITED

Taking Paganism Beyond the Circle

Gede Parma

A new generation of Pagan youth is here, and now there is a book that uniquely heralds their arrival. *Spirited* speaks directly to the young adult set, offering an incisive look at the complex issues that they face on the Path. This book addresses everything that a young Pagan deals with in daily life, from school and social life to friends and family to sexuality and love. Contemporary Pagan issues and spiritual practices are also discussed, including ethics, spellcraft, ritual, divinity, tradition, covencraft, and solitary work.

Interwoven with stories, advice, and firsthand experiences from young Pagans who've "been there, done that," progressive Pagans of any age will welcome this dynamic and compassionate guide to Pagan living.

978-0-7387-1507-0

$18.95, 6 x 9, 336 pp.

index

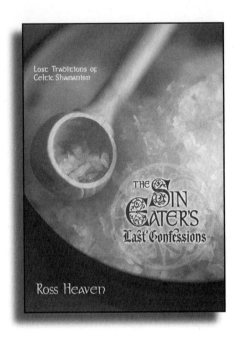

Lost Traditions of
Celtic Shamanism

THE SIN
EATER'S
Last Confessions

Ross Heaven

The Sin Eater's Last Confessions

Lost Traditions of Celtic Shamanism

Ross Heaven

Considered a madman in his English village, Adam Dilwyn Vaughan—a sin eater—was shunned by the same community who flocked to him for healing. This true tale records Ross Heaven's fascinating journey as the sin eater's apprentice, who is introduced to the lost art of sin eating and other Celtic shamanic traditions.

This spiritual memoir records the author's wondrous and moving experiences with the powerful energies of the natural world. He witnesses Adam removing negative energies from a patient, meets fairy folk, reads omens in nature, discovers his soul purpose through dreaming, goes on a vision quest in a sacred cave, and participates in a sin eating ritual. Interlacing these remarkable events are Welsh legends and enlightening discussions that shed light on these mysterious practices and invite you to see the world through the eyes of a shaman.

Also included is a sin eater's workbook of the same shamanic exercises and techniques practiced by Adam.

978-0-7387-1356-4

$16.95, 5 x 7, 288 pp.

bibliography, references

TO ORDER, CALL 1-877-NEW-WRLD
Prices subject to change without notice
Order at Llewellyn.com 24 hours a day, 7 days a week!

TO WRITE TO THE AUTHOR

If you wish to contact the author or would like more information about this book, please write to the author in care of Llewellyn Worldwide, and we will forward your request. Both the author and publisher appreciate hearing from you and learning of your enjoyment of this book and how it has helped you. Llewellyn Worldwide cannot guarantee that every letter written to the author can be answered, but all will be forwarded. Please write to:

Gede Parma
℅ Llewellyn Worldwide
2143 Wooddale Drive
Woodbury, MN 55125-2989

Please enclose a self-addressed stamped envelope for reply,
or $1.00 to cover costs. If outside U.S.A., enclose
international postal reply coupon.

Many of Llewellyn's authors have websites with additional information and resources. For more information, please visit our website:

http://www.llewellyn.com